The
Princeton
Review

8 STEPS TO HELP BLACK FAMILIES PAY FOR COLLEGE

A CRASH COURSE IN FINANCIAL AID

Thomas LaVeist, Ph.D. and Will LaVeist

Random House, Inc.
New York
www.PrincetonReview.com

Princeton Review Publishing, L. L. C.
2315 Broadway
New York, NY 10024
E-mail: bookeditor@review.com

ISBN 0-375-76306-6

Editorial Director: Robert Franek
Editors: Erica Magrey and Margo Orlando
Designer: Scott Harris
Production Editor: Julieanna Lambert
Production Coordinator: Greta Englert

Manufactured in the United States of America.

9 8 7 6 5 4 3 2 1

ACKNOWLEDGMENTS

We are eternally grateful to God, who continues to provide us with more grace than we ask for, while never allowing us to face more trouble than we can handle.

We are also grateful to the members of our committee of African American financial aid officers and advisors, who provided us with important advice and feedback, as well as encouragement and constructive criticism, which was precisely what we needed at various points in the process. They were also invaluable resources in helping us gain access to other experts, all of whom graciously agreed to help us. Their names are: Kevin Cuffie, Lynn Drummond, Mark Gay, Gerry Lovick, Jean Richie, Jamie T. McMillan, Curry Greene, and William Barber.

We are particularly indebted to financial aid consultant Kalman Chany for his many financial aid insights and to Tamyra Carroll for her research assistance and student perspective. We also owe a debt of gratitude to David Brand and Tom Joyner, who convinced us to write this book. Of course, this book would not have been possible without the understanding and patience of our wives, Bridgette and Rita. Rita delayed celebration of her tenth wedding anniversary while we pulled an all-night writing session to get the book finished!

The real stars of this book are our sons Carlton and Daniel. Together with our other children, Randall, Joshua, Coryn, Naomi, and Clay, they motivate us to strive for excellence each day and to be loving parents who stress the importance of education in the way that our parents William and Eudora did.

CONTENTS

FOREWORD

I'm excited about any tool designed to help black kids get an education. And a book geared toward helping black families pay for their kids' education—that's almost too good to be true. If you know anything about me, aside from being the Hardest Working Man in Radio, I, through the Tom Joyner Foundation, am also the Hardest Working Fundraiser for kids attending Historically Black Colleges and Universities. Why? Because I know how tough it is for students to have to return home from college without attaining their degree, not because they were poor students but simply because they don't have the funds needed to continue their education. That's a crime, not just for the poor student who has to try to adjust to life back at home, but for the parents too. They've bragged about June Bug. They've bought June Bug a stereo system and a nice set of twin sheets. They've turned June Bug's room into a den!

I have a strong belief that *every* student who wishes to attend college should have the opportunity to do so.

I was not the best student in the world, but the things I did gain in my five years at Tuskegee University in Alabama (and yes I did say five years) was a sense of pride in what black people like me were able to accomplish, a sense of the university's rich history, and a heightened level of confidence in what I could achieve in the future. It's also my belief that Historically Black Colleges and Universities offer African American students the kind of nurturing environment that they are often unable to receive at mainstream institutions. I wish every black kid could go to an HBCU, but that's a lot to ask, even for a big dreamer like me.

But whether you or your children are applying to an HBCU or an Ivy League College, it's going to take money, and *8 Steps to Help Black Families Pay for College: A Crash Course in Financial Aid,* is a must read. In fact, I would recommend this book to people with very young children so that by the time their children are ready to go to college, they will already have a clear understanding of how much money they need, and most importantly, where they're going to get it. Choosing the right school, where to go for financial aid, and how to keep from getting into debt are just a few of the topics that are covered in this book.

How many people do you know that have graduated from college in a mountain of debt that's almost impossible to pay off? They spend years either making monthly loan payments or dodging collection phone calls from the government. We send our children to college to get an education that will improve their lives. But how productive can they be if they're broke, in debt, and have horrible credit, often before they land their first real jobs? This cycle has got to end. Educating parents about how to keep their children from making bad financial choices is a step toward changing the tide.

The Tom Joyner Foundation tries to help as many students as it can, but for those of you who want to help yourselves, I suggest that you read this book long before you make any major renovations to your child's bedroom. If you aren't prepared financially in a world of ever-rising costs in tuition, housing, and books, your kid may be returning home from college a lot sooner than you had anticipated . . . with that loud stereo equipment you bought her! Read this book with your child so he or she can learn along with you; then when you're finished, have your child test you to see how well you've done. Of course the greatest reward will be watching your child receive his or her college degree, knowing that you used this common-sense guide to make it happen without going bankrupt in the process.

Education is a beautiful thing, and money (or the lack of it) should never be the deciding factor on whether our children attend college. Unfortunately, it often is. It's up to us to use all the tools that we have to make sure they have the finances needed to advance. Your child may be able to contribute to humanity the way Dr. Martin Luther King did, to science the way George Washington Carver did, to journalism the way Ed Bradley is doing, or to sports like Steve "Air" McNair. These HBCU graduates have given great things to the world. Let's not let our inability to follow a good financial plan for their education stifle the future contributions of our kids. Let's teach our kids how to have financial freedom. That's a gift that money can't buy.

TOM JOYNER
October 2002

INTRODUCTION

We've all made decisions based on "They say . . . ." We embrace as law outside advice on topics we don't know much about. And we're especially vulnerable to "They say . . ." when we're faced with stressful issues that affect our future, like what college to attend and how to pay for it.

The phantom self-proclaimed "experts" of "They say . . ." *seem* to know a lot about the college application process and about getting financial aid. They try to predict how our sacrifices and rewards will balance out in the future. "Forget about getting financial aid. Your mom and dad make way too much money," *they* say discouragingly. Are slim paychecks the problem? *They* seem to have some words of wisdom on that issue, too: "Haven't you heard affirmative action is over? Forget minority scholarships. These days a black man or woman can't pay for their kid's college unless they make at least six figures." As soon as somebody mentions student loans, all hell breaks loose. What do *they* have to say about loans? "Not me! I wouldn't do it. You want to be paying those things back for the rest of your life? You're better off not going to school."

But what do *they* know, anyway?

Did *they* graduate from college? Do *they* really have your best interests at heart?

Congratulations: picking up this book proves you've realized that it's time to stop leaning on the unreliable opinions of others and start arming yourself with the information you need to pay for college. What *they* don't realize is that regardless of your income, a college degree is attainable. You just have to be willing to work hard and smart to reach your goal. This book will help you do just that.

We are not financial aid officers. We are two brothers—a university professor and an accomplished journalist—with college-bound teenage sons. We know a lot about financial aid now, but we weren't always experts on this topic. The turning point was a conversation between the two of us at a family reunion about how we intended to finance our sons' educations. We talked about the information we had gathered from the books we'd read and websites we'd visited, and we realized that there was still a lot we didn't know. We had figured that because we went to undergrad and graduate schools and had been through the financial aid process ourselves, we would have a handle on college financing. Well, we were wrong. A lot has changed since we were in school more than ten years ago, and even then, we didn't know all the ins and outs. So there we were—two fathers, both professionally trained to ask questions and find answers—without the information we needed to get us through this confusing process. We imagined how difficult it must be for *other* African American parents of high school students who are wondering how *they* will pay for college—parents who might not have the same easy access to information that we have. That's when we decided to join forces and write this book to help clear the noise about financial aid.

We wrote this book as a resource for African American families, and it deals specifically with some of the cultural issues and concerns black families may have regarding college financing. We got the real 411 from African American financial aid officers and advisors from major colleges and universities in the United

States. Thanks to their advice and reflections, you'll get a handle on how to navigate the financial aid process so you get the financial aid package that you deserve.

Parents: Whether you began saving for college when your high school senior was wearing diapers or you just began thinking about it today, this book can help you make the right moves. And students, listen up: This book is for you, too. There are plenty of things you can do to help your parents with financial aid, so make sure you pay attention to what's going on here.

We may address certain sections to students or parents, but our advice is generally appropriate for both students *and* parents. We believe families should go through the college selection, application, and financial aid processes together—discuss, question, and investigate these new worlds as a team. The decisions that students or parents make about college affect the entire family.

We use eight simple steps to clarify the process of understanding and applying for financial aid:

Step 1: *Get Your Mind Right*

We'll address the potentially harmful attitudes that African Americans may have toward money, and we'll emphasize how important college really is— and that the sacrifices are worth it.

Step 2: *Choose the Right School*

We'll discuss how to assess the student's needs and select schools that will best serve those needs. We'll also address the "right" and "wrong" reasons to select a school—we've heard a lot of crazy reasons over the years!

Step 3: *Get Your Head Around Financial Aid*

We'll explain how your expected family contribution (EFC) is calculated, and we'll unlock the mystery of all the different types of available aid. We'll also dispel some common myths about financial aid.

Step 4: *Learn How to Get the Financial Aid You Need and Deserve*

We'll offer some tips for lowering your EFC, and we'll let you know what the student can do to earn more financial aid.

Step 5: *Apply for Aid*

We'll spell out the process step by step and show you some mistakes to avoid. We'll also pass on some real-life stories of how other African American families fared.

Step 6: *Assess and Respond to the Financial Aid Offer*

You don't have to accept the first package that comes your way. We'll show you how to negotiate a better deal.

Step 7: *What Happens During College?*

For each year the student attends college, you'll have to go through the financial aid process. We'll give you an idea of what to expect and what may change over the years.

Step 8: *Give Back*

Repaying student loans is essential to protect your credit rating and lower your school's default rate; we'll give you the options you have for paying it back. We'll also stress the importance of donating to your alma mater and worthy charitable organizations.

After digesting these eight simple steps, you'll have enough financial savvy to make smart choices about financing a college education. You might also want to refer to The Princeton Review's *Paying for College Without Going Broke* for more in-depth information on this subject. This book is meant to be a resource for you throughout the college years, and even afterward. Who knows—with this much knowledge at your fingertips, you might even help college-bound friends and family to escape the trap of "They say . . . ."

This is an exciting time for your family, and we hope this book helps demystify the financial aid process.

STEP 1: GET YOUR MIND RIGHT

Remember the family reunion we mentioned earlier, where we decided to write this book? That very same day, a hip-hop song on the radio triggered a talk with our sons about money. Over the thumping bass and between a few lyrics we couldn't quite make out, the rapper hollered, "Bling bling!" We're not *that* out of touch, so we knew what the phrase meant. But we asked our sons what "bling bling" was all about anyway.

With the belief that they were teaching *us* a lesson for a change, they confidently explained that "bling bling" referred to the jewelry that many rappers flaunt, especially large gold or platinum pendants, and diamond rings. We asked them, "If you see a person who is bling blinging, does this mean they're wealthy?" They looked at us as if we had asked a stupid question, and then they winked at each other. "Of course," they answered. "How could they buy all that jewelry, the cars, and the fresh clothes they wear if they didn't have money?" But there's a huge difference between having money to spend—and having wealth to pass on.

Wouldn't it be great to be able to write the college a check each year and be done with it? Wouldn't it be great to not have to bother with financial aid at all? Any parent would be proud to be able to provide their child with the full tuition to the school of his or her choice. Some Americans do pay for college this way, but it's not an option for most parents. Many of us aren't able to put aside a chunk of money each year and accept the fact that we are kissing away upward of $100,000 for four or more years of schooling. Some of us can't afford to save money or invest sizeable funds, but more often, we just don't get around to doing it.

If we really want to "keep it real," we need to admit that many African Americans—regardless of income, regardless of who is "bling blinging" and who isn't—have a problem taking care of money. Now, if you are beginning to feel like we are about to get too far up in your business, you definitely need to read this chapter. For those of you who already have your minds right—meaning, you are spending wisely, investing, and building true wealth that you will pass on to your children—we applaud you. For those of you who didn't start saving and investing early, have high debts, or have high income but no money saved, keep reading—we'll show you that paying for college is still doable.

FIRST, LET'S LOOK AT THE PRICE TAG

As you well know, parents and students are expected to contribute to the cost of attending college, and many families are nervous about exactly how much that contribution is going to be. But a college education is still considered crucial, particularly for African Americans who want to move on up and become competitive in today's workforce. One of the most obvious advantages of earning a college degree is advanced earning potential. But unfortunately, tuition and income are not increasing at the same rate.

Over the past few decades, college costs have skyrocketed. In the late 1970s, a college education was doable for around $1,000 to $2,000 a year at a public school, and $6,000 to $9,000 at a private school. According to The College Board, in the 2002–2003 school year, the average cost of a four-year private college is $18,273 (a 5.8 percent increase from last year). A four-year public school was $4,081 (a 9.6 percent increase from last year).

A 2002 report titled *Losing Ground,* by The National Center for Public Policy and Higher Education, showed that families are spending higher portions of their annual income to cover college costs. Focusing on public colleges and universities, the report said that the portion of income that low- and middle-income families were spending on tuition had increased from only 13 percent in 1980 to 25 percent in the 2000–2001 school year. From 1992 to 2001, tuition rose faster than family income in 41 states. Concerning financial aid, the report said that though federal and state governments have increased the amount of money they contribute to college education, these increases have not kept pace with tuition either. Grant aid diminished significantly between 1986 and 1999: the average federal Pell Grant went from covering 98 percent of tuition to only 57 percent, while state aid coverage dropped from 75 percent to 64 percent.

Accompanying this decrease in grant aid is an increase in the percentage of students borrowing money to pay for college. In 1981, loans accounted for approximately 45 percent of financial aid and grants accounted for 52 percent; in 2000, loans accounted for 58 percent, whereas grants covered only 45 percent of financial aid packages. This shift toward replacing grants with loans to cover a student's financial need has contributed to higher debt burden among recent graduates.

However, though the reality of covering college costs can be tough, the outlook is far from being all gloom and doom. The most recent 2002–2003 school year figures from the College Board show that 38 percent of students at four-year schools actually pay less than $4,000 for tuition and fees. Nearly 70 percent of students pay less than $8,000 for tuition, and only 7 percent of all students attend schools that have tuition tabs of $24,000 or more. About 75 percent of all students at four-year private schools and 60 percent of those at public schools receive financial aid. Still . . .

ANY WAY YOU SLICE IT, IT'S A LOT OF MONEY

And that's what financial aid is for. Read on.

GET YOUR MIND RIGHT—FROM THE BEGINNING

Parents: You can and should start saving when your children are young. Saving, of course, means *not spending*. A study conducted by The Selig Center of the University of Georgia's Terry School of Business estimated the spending power of African Americans at $588.7 billion per year in 2000 and $645.9 billion in 2002. We have all this money flowing through our hands, yet we lack wealth compared to other groups because we spend more than we keep. Census data from 2000 shows the median household income (meaning half of the household incomes were above this amount, and half were below) at $30,436 for African Americans, and $44,232 for the average white household. Census data from 1995 (the most recent year available for this particular data) indicates that black households have a median net worth (assets minus debt) of $7,073. Meanwhile, white households have a median net worth of

$49,030. While African American income is 68.9 percent of white income, our net worth is only 14.4 percent of white net worth! At the end of the day, we might *own* a lot—but many of us don't have jack when it comes to paying for college or other major expenses.

We are not trying to ignore the long history of slavery, oppression, and discrimination that contributes to this disparity, but history is only one part of the equation. One of the main reasons that net worth is so low for so many of us is that we have the wrong ideas about money. For example, many people don't understand the difference between income and wealth. Income can create wealth over time—but your weekly paycheck shouldn't be seen as immediate profit. Instead, you can manipulate and control how you spend your income to *build* wealth. Income can also include profits made from investments or the sale of goods or property, all of which can eventually contribute to wealth. If you're spending as much as you're making, you're preventing your funds from accumulating.

THE BOTTOM LINE

The first step in managing your money is learning how to distinguish between the different aspects of your finances. To measure profits and losses, businesses use a balance sheet, which is a document that illustrates how the business's money is distributed between income, expenses, assets, and liabilities, to reveal cash flow and net worth. You can use a balance sheet to evaluate your personal financial situation as well. Two of the most important lines on a balance sheet are the top line and the bottom line. The top line shows your salary and income—the total amount of money you make. The bottom line shows what's left after you've paid taxes, expenses, and so on. African Americans tend to focus on the wrong line—the top line. We like to be able to say how big our paychecks are. But what's the sense of making $95,000 a year when you still have as much trouble paying your bills as does someone who earns $15,000 a year and has a family of five? When planning for college, you should focus on the bottom line, which shows how much money you have to invest and save.

THE JOHNSON FAMILY FINANCIAL STATEMENTS

The Johnson family is a typical African American middle-class family. Mr. and Mrs. Johnson have a combined annual income of $110,000. According to the U.S. Census Bureau, in 2000, the median family income for the nation (all race groups) was $50,890. While the Johnson's have a high combined income, they have a very troubling bottom line. With only $122 left over at the end of the month, there isn't much room for error, is there?

When you look at the Johnsons' income statement you see that they have made a few classic financial mistakes that led to a shaky financial situation. Let us point out a few of these mistakes.

First, they have far too much credit card debt. They are spending $1,140 per month financing these cards. This is a serious amount of money when you consider that instead of each monthly payment directly cutting down the original amount of debt, it's also going toward the interest on that debt.

A second classic mistake is the price tag of the cars they drive. Someone told them that they could have a lower monthly car payment and a smaller down payment if they leased a car rather than buying one. This was true, but it hasn't worked out to their advantage. The car they are financing cost $38,000 when they bought it; now it's worth much less ($24,000), yet they owe more ($31,000) than it is worth. How did they get so deep in debt? They didn't have a car to trade in when they purchased the new car because they had leased their previous car.

Johnson Family Monthly Income Statement	
Income	
Salary (gross)	$9,167
Total Income	**$9,167**
Expenses	
Taxes	$1,980
Visa	$350
Mastercard	$320
Discover card	$285
Department store credit card	$185
Home mortgage	$1,965
Second mortgage	$675
Auto loan	$625
Auto lease	$475
Food	$900
Clothes	$600
Utilities	$475
Telephone, Internet, cable TV	$210
Savings	Whatever is left over
Total Expenses	**$9,045**
Monthly Cash Flow (Income – Expenses = Cash Flow)	**$122**

What's the big deal about having a $31,000 auto loan? The big deal is that financial aid formulas don't consider auto loans as debt, so the federal processor, and the financial aid officer at each of the schools applied to will think the Johnsons have $31,000 more to spend than they actually do. The value of a car is *not* considered an asset under either federal or school financial aid formulas.

Johnson Family Balance Sheet

Assets	
Savings	$2,200
Stocks	$0
Bonds	$0
Receivables	$0
Home value	$295,000
Other property	$13,000
Car value	$24,400
Total Assets	**$334,600**
Liabilities	
Home mortgage balance	$232,000
Second mortgage	$48,000
Visa	$12,750
Mastercard	$10,125
Discover card	$7,325
Auto loan	$31,000
Remaining car-lease payments	$11,400
Total Liabilities	**$352,600**
Net Worth **(Assets – Liabilities = Net Worth)**	**–$18,000**

The only significant asset the Johnsons own is their home, but cousin *They-say* told them that they should take some equity out of their home to pay down some of their debt and take a nice vacation. And although the cruise was nice, the Johnsons now have to pay the piper to the tune of a $48,000 second mortgage with a $675 monthly payment. And naturally, they ran those credit cards right back up to the max again.

The Johnsons are paying $2,915 per month toward their debt (not including their primary mortgage). This is $34,980 per year, which is 40.56 percent of their annual after-tax income. And guess what: Financial aid does not take most debts into consideration!

Many of us have a dependable income but are in a financial hole. We get into this hole because we work hard for our money and then don't allow our money to work hard for us. When payday comes, we make bad decisions. When we get a salary increase, we spend more or take on additional expenses. We buy a new car and a bigger house because someone (there goes "They say . . ." again) told us that we needed a bigger tax write-off. But after buying that bigger house we find that what we got in return was a higher mortgage payment and less money at the end of the month. So, as our salaries increase, our debt-to-income ratio increases along with it. We may look as if we are "bling blinging," when the reality is much, much different.

Many of us fail to invest whatever we can. We don't want to be "left behind," so we pursue the illusion of wealth. We charge clothes, food, and expensive items such as big screen TVs. We even go to restaurants and charge the meal. Instead of paying the bill immediately, we end up paying interest on a meal we ate and digested months ago! Then we try to hit "the big one" by religiously playing the state lottery or the numbers each week. (We admit we've bought a few lottery tickets over the years too. It's hard to resist plunking down $1 for a chance at $20 million!)

So what's the solution? How do you get out of the rat race of working hard for mo' money, only to see it disappear in taxes, high interest debts, and foolish spending, continuing the seemingly endless downward spiral? Get a financial plan. Stop spending and charging items you don't really need. Pay off your credit cards every month. Get your mind right about money.

GET YOUR MIND RIGHT ABOUT COLLEGE

As you have probably heard, enrollment in U.S. colleges is growing steadily. What you may not know is that the bulk of new students will be minorities, most of whom are first-generation college students.

In the 1999–2000 school year, African American students made up only 13 percent of all undergraduates. Despite these numbers, African Americans have the right attitude about college. According to a study from 2000 titled *Great Expectations: How the Public and Parents—White, African American and Hispanic— View Higher Education*, by John Immerwahr of Villanova University, 47 percent of black parents of high school students believe that college is the single most important factor necessary for success in today's work world, as do 65 percent of Hispanic parents, yet only 33 percent of white parents believe as much. But in contrast, among eighteen- to twenty-four-year-olds, only 20 percent of Hispanic Americans are enrolled in higher education, compared to 30 percent of African Americans and 37 percent of whites.

Since you're reading this book, you probably realize that college really does make a difference—and we applaud you. Plenty of people make it without a degree, but in general, according to the State PIRG's (Public Interest Research Group) Higher Education Project, a bachelor's degree is "worth" about 75 percent more than a high school diploma, or more than $1,000,000 over a lifetime in the workforce. That's a lot of money, considering that 22 percent of African American undergraduates enrolled during the 1999–2000 school year came from families that made less than $20,000 annually.

Doubt that college will help you to succeed? One of the key reasons wealth eludes us is that many of us lack patience. We want the big house and the fancy car now. This mindset has many African American young people forgoing college because they believe obtaining a college degree takes too long. They see professional ballplayers, rappers, and singers getting paid right out of high school without having a college education, and they don't realize that this is not the norm. Here's something you already know but may not want to admit: Because of the stiff competition and limited slots on each team or at a record label, it's much more difficult to become a successful NBA basketball player or chart-topping re-cording artist than it is to earn a college degree.

We live in a celebrity culture, and it's easy to get swept up in chasing our own "fifteen minutes." It seems as if anyone, at any time, could be *the next big thing*. Why not us? It might be tough to see rich and famous eighteen-year-olds with their cars and clothes, and compare that to the life *you'll* probably lead at age eighteen: heavy books, hours of studying, greasy pizza delivered to your dorm room at midnight. Why "settle" for *this*?

We won't deny that you can get a job and "make it" without going to college. The 1990s produced many entrepreneurs who became millionaires without attending or finishing college or obtaining professional degrees. Getting a college degree, however, significantly increases your chances of success in your career and finances. So before you decide to skip college for that great job, consider the benefits of donning the cap and gown.

COLLEGE COUNTS

College is an amazing experience that graduates often reflect upon with feelings of intense warmth and nostalgia. The college years are said to be among the best in your life, and it's no wonder—where else can you dive into subjects you really love, become part of a community of people your own age with similar goals and interests, and make friends that you'll keep for the rest of your life?

If the sheer desire for knowledge and adventure isn't enough incentive, maybe these figures will spark your interest: According to data from the U.S. Census Bureau, the median income in 1999 for an African American male aged twenty-five to thirty-four with at least a bachelor's degree was $47,515. For an African American male with just a high school diploma or GED, it was $29,162. That's a difference of $18,353 each year. For males between the ages of thirty-five and forty-four, the difference in median income was $28,874.

For African American women, the numbers look like this: The median income for an African American female age twenty-five to thirty-four with a high school diploma is $17,373, and for a college graduate, it's $31,916; that's a difference of $13,950. For women between the ages of thirty-five and forty-four, the difference is $16,417. In the long run, it pays to go to college.

GET YOUR MIND RIGHT ABOUT DEBT

We often hear people say they have no interest in going to college because they don't want to be paying back loans for years and years. But don't many of us feel this same financial burden paying hundreds of dollars a month to credit card companies, trying to chip away at plastic debt? Taking out loans to finance college is a smart money move, and nothing you can buy with a credit card compares to the value of your higher education.

There is good debt, and then there is bad debt.

STUDENT LOANS = GOOD DEBT

Student loans represent an investment in YOU. Your college education is one of the most important investments you'll ever make—it will last you a lifetime. Your education is *worth* being in debt for.

The interest rates on student loans are typically much lower than on other types of consumer loans. On July 1, 2002, student loan rates dropped to the lowest levels ever. Because of rule changes voted on by Congress, the interest rate for Stafford Loans fell from 5.99 percent to 4.06 percent, and the rate for PLUS loans dropped from 6.79 percent to 4.86 percent. (We'll explain the different types of loans in Step 3.) Graduating students and those who graduated but had not already consolidated their loans were able to begin repaying their loans at these new rates. Your education will likely lead to a higher salary, which should enable you to repay the loans and maintain a higher standard of living than you would have had if you had not graduated from college.

A Friendly Reminder

Student loans, like credit cards, are not free money. Six months after you graduate, drop below half-time enrollment, or drop out, you will have to begin repaying your loans with interest. It's not easy. We know; we've been out of college for more than ten years now. Thomas was able to pay off his loans early by doubling up on the payments. Will is still paying his loans. Knowing what we know now, would we take out student loans to finance our college education if we had to do it all over again? Absolutely. Each of us enjoys a more comfortable lifestyle and standard of living than we did growing up in "the projects" in Brownsville, Brooklyn, New York. Believing in good debt made college possible.

It's important to remember that student loans involve both the parents and the student. These loans usually make up a large part of a financial package and affect the parents while the student is in school. But they're called "student loans" for a reason—you, the student, is the borrower, and repayment is your responsibility. Parents and students should discuss loans together. Everyone should be involved and aware of what sort of debt you're taking on. (We'll talk more about the specifics of student loan debts for African Americans in Step 8.)

CREDIT CARD ABUSE = BAD DEBT

Now on to bad debt, and one of its classic causes: the irresponsible use of credit cards. According to Nellie Mae, a provider of federal and private education loans, credit card use among college students increased by 24 percent between 1998 and 2001. Eighty-three percent of undergraduates have credit cards, and 54 percent of freshmen have them; the average credit card debt level among undergrads is $2,327. Nellie Mae also reports that the average combined student loan and credit card debt for graduating seniors is $20,402. With credit card interest rates averaging 18.9 percent, the debt burden students may face after graduation is scary.

We've been conditioned to believe that receiving a credit card is a rite of passage, signaling that we have "arrived." But credit cards can get you into a heap of trouble if you don't know how to use them wisely—that is, charge within your means, and pay off your balance each month.

One of the biggest mistakes students (and plenty of other credit card holders) make is that they pay only the minimum amount due each month. If you adopt this plan of action, your balance will continue to grow and you'll spend all your money on the interest that is accumulating.

IT'S BETTER TO INVEST

So instead of paying credit card companies money that you don't even have, pay yourself. Save and invest 10 to 15 percent of what you make. Invest in the stock market, in solid companies that have been around for years and whose products you use and understand. Prepare for your retirement by investing in IRAs and your employer's 401(k) plan, where the company will match your contribution.

TAKE CONTROL OF YOUR FINANCES

Educating yourself about money is a big part of preparing for the college years. In addition to reading this book, you might consider reading money management and investment magazines such as *Black Enterprise*, which will help educate you about investing and offer tips that match your financial situation. The CEO and publisher of *Black Enterprise,* Earl G. Graves, serves as an inspiration to the black community. Among scores of accomplishments, he was named one of the ten most outstanding minority businessmen in the country in 1972 by President Nixon.

Black Enterprise also has a wealth-building kit that can help you get started. Inside the kit is a document called the Declaration of Financial Empowerment (DOFE). This document highlights the ten principles of financial empowerment brought to you by the Black Wealth Initiative, a campaign that aims to enhance your financial potential.

The declaration includes one principle dedicated to teaching financial empowerment to your children—a vital subject that is not taught in schools. When we were teens like our sons, we didn't understand the difference between having money to spend and money to pass on. This is one of the most important life lessons a parent can teach a child. But in order to do this, each parent must first get his or her *own* mind right. It will be a costly mistake if you don't.

To find out more about the DOFE and other steps to financial fitness, visit **www.blackenterprise.com/WBK.asp**.

**TODAY IS THE DAY I TAKE CONTROL
OF MY FINANCIAL DESTINY.**

Black Enterprise

**DECLARATION OF
FINANCIAL EMPOWERMENT**

In order to attain a measure of success, power and wealth, I shall uphold the principles of saving and investing as well as controlled spending and disciplined consumerism. I vow to fully participate in the capital markets and make a solid commitment to a program of wealth accumulation. Determination and consistency will serve as my guides, and I shall not allow external or internal forces to keep me from reaching my goals. By adjusting my course and embracing a new mandate that stresses planning, education and fortitude, I lay a strong, unbreakable foundation for the preservation and enrichment of my family, children and children's children.

I,_____ , from this day forward, declare my vigilant and life-long commitment to financial empowerment. I pledge the following:

1. To save and invest 10% to 15% of my after-tax income

2. To be a proactive and informed investor

3. To be a disciplined and knowledgeable consumer

4. To measure my personal wealth by net worth, not income

5. To engage in sound budget, credit and tax management practices

6. To teach business and financial principles to my children

7. To use a portion of my personal wealth to strengthen my community

8. To support the creation and growth of profitable, competitive blackowned enterprises

9. To maximize my earning power through a commitment to career development, technological literacy and professional excellence

10. To ensure that my wealth is passed on to future generations.

I have committed to this unwavering, personal covenant as a means of bolstering myself, my family and my community. In adopting this resolution, I intend to use all available resources, wisdom and power to gain my share of the American Dream.

Agreed and signed: _____ Date:_____

To commit and get your wealth building guide, go to
http://www.blackenterprise.com/Investing/20.htm.

AFFIRMATIVE ACTION, COLLEGE ADMISSIONS, AND FINANCIAL AID

Affirmative action: it's a pretty loaded phrase, isn't it? Chances are you can't read these words together without calling to mind a specific case or debate you read about. We're not going to give you an extended treatise on what makes affirmative action good or bad—that's a conversation that could go on all night. What we will give you is an overview of how affirmative action affects you right here, right now—when you're applying for college and for financial aid.

First of all, what *is* affirmative action? Like so many words and phrases, *affirmative action* has been tossed around pretty carelessly over the past few years, and its actual meaning has been blurred, if not lost altogether. Contrary to what you may have heard (contrary to what "They say . . ."!), affirmative action is not about quotas—that is, it's not meant to force schools or businesses into accepting or hiring a certain percentage of minorities or women. Instead, affirmative action is meant to level the playing field and ensure that schools and businesses are not intentionally discriminating against minority groups. Let's look at colleges as an example: Around 12 percent of all college students are black; if the student body at your college is only 1 percent black, it's likely that there is some discrimination at work. Now, this isn't always the case, of course—but it's the principle that affirmative action was built on. When discrimination is suspected, schools or businesses should make special efforts to reach new pools of minority applicants in an effort to diversify their staff or student body. Affirmative action is meant simply to help minorities overcome past discrimination and achieve a level of diversity that many people argue is essential in higher education.

Misperceptions

One common misperception about affirmative action is that it allows less-qualified people to "take the place" of those who are more qualified (but who happen to be white males). When affirmative action works the way it's supposed to, this isn't the case, and those hired or accepted should be as qualified as anyone else.

When it comes to affirmative action and college admissions, the process gets tricky. Unlike jobs, in which the requirements a candidate must meet are pretty straightforward, the requirements for admission to a college aren't so clear-cut. A college application is made up of many components, all of which are important—your SAT scores, your high school transcript, your essays, your extracurricular activities, your personal interviews. Which of these components is the most important? Ask ten different people and you'll most likely get ten different answers. Admissions officers at ten different schools might have ten different answers, too. In the landmark court case of 1978, *Regents of the University of California v. Bakke*, it was decided that race could be one of the components taken into account. (This legal precedent has often been challenged, and many colleges are reconsidering—or being forced to reconsider—their use of race in admissions.)

Many schools rightly believe that diversity is an important part of an education, and actively seek to attract minority students. Sometimes these minorities have lower grade point averages or SAT scores than nonminorities. Sometimes, however, so do athletes, artists, musicians, children of alumni (legacies), people who have shown their commitment to volunteer work, or people who have overcome serious obstacles in life. Is someone with a higher GPA or SAT score "more qualified" for college than one of these people? Of course not. Colleges, that is, *selective* colleges, admit students whom they think offer something to the university. These colleges aren't so much concerned with admitting well-rounded students as they are with building well-rounded classes. Admissions officers are looking for students from a variety of backgrounds who have a variety of talents.

Look Out for "They Say . . . "

According to the Department of Education's National Center for Education Statistics, out of the 16.5 million undergrads in 1999–2000, more than a third were earning grades of C or lower. And of all African American students, 48.9 percent fell into this category—a larger percentage than in any other group. Opponents of affirmative action sometimes use statistics like these to make the case that certain ethnic groups are "in over their heads" when it comes to college. Does this figure really mean that affirmative action is doing colleges a disservice? Not at all. The executive director of the National Association of Scholars, Bradford P. Wilson, explains it this way: "The most obvious thing that it suggests is that African Americans are coming to colleges and universities with less preparation for college-level work than other groups. But I wouldn't blame it on affirmative action, because most of the institutions [included in the report] are not selective institutions." Poor grades can be a reflection of any number of cultural, personal, or academic factors.

Affirmative Action and Financial Aid

As for financial aid, it only makes sense that colleges will do their best to meet the financial need of the students they want the most, whether those students are African American, white, Hispanic, or another ethnicity. Many minorities do indeed come from families with low incomes, and if a school is committed to improving its minority representation, one good way to do so is to make sure minority students receive the money they need to attend. Despite this fact, race-targeted financial aid is unusual at most schools, and schools that have tried to use it (such as Northern Virginia Community College, which had privately funded minority scholarships) have been taken to court. Financial aid will be based on what your family can afford to pay. Affirmative action will not really play a role.

RECENT CONFLICTS WITH AFFIRMATIVE ACTION

At the time of this writing, there are several big court cases regarding the constitutionality of using affirmative action with college admissions. Many of these cases are based on reverse-discrimination charges—that is, charges that the admissions criteria give preference to minorities, in effect discriminating against white students. It's difficult to determine what these conflicts will mean for you—it all depends on where you live and where you're planning to apply. In Texas, for example, using race in college admissions is prohibited, but an "alternative" to affirmative action has been implemented: students in the top 10 percent of their class in every high school in the state are automatically accepted into the University of Texas school system. Similar plans are in effect in California (top 4 percent of students) and Florida (top 20 percent of students). Though the Texas plan is four years old now, it's coming under scrutiny because Texas A&M University wants to admit students in the top 20 percent of "low-performing" high schools. Does this mean that more underprivileged minorities will be given a chance they might not otherwise have, or does it mean that underqualified students will be "taking the place" of more qualified applicants? There's no easy answer, nor should there be. The issue of fairness is complex, and what's "fair" or "unfair" must sometimes be determined on a case-by-case basis.

What's most important to keep in mind here is that affirmative action is neither out to hurt you nor out to give you something you don't deserve. One thing is certain: No college is permitted to have separate admissions criteria for different racial groups; all students must be in competition with one another regardless of race. Affirmative action is meant, as we said, to ensure that the doors of higher education are open to everyone. Don't worry about being accepted into a college "because you're black." As we said, there are many, many components to a college application that are weighed differently for each student, and your application will be evaluated for its merit and strength just like any other.

This is a case where listening to "They say . . . " could really set you on the wrong path, and it's what has blurred the true intentions of affirmative action in the first place. What you need to keep in mind is that affirmative action aims for equal opportunity and equal access for everyone.

STEP 2: CHOOSE THE RIGHT SCHOOL

Having grown up in New York City, the Mecca of basketball, we are huge hoops fans. So when "March Madness" comes around, we get caught up in the hype that grips college basketball followers. "March Madness," the term basketball afficionados use to describe the annual NCAA basketball tournament, determines college basketball's national champion. Fans are psyched for three solid weekends of thrilling games, alumni are energized at the prospect of winning bragging rights over other colleges, and money flows back to the schools' athletic programs. There is also another lesser-known form of "madness" that happens every year: the college whose team wins the championship can expect the number of admissions applications to skyrocket the following year. After all, a televised basketball game is like a national two-hour commercial in prime time. But are "commercials" a good way to select a college? We think not.

There are more than 4,600 higher education institutions in the United States. With so many options out there, you can be relatively certain that there's a "right" college for everyone. Finding the "right" college for you isn't always easy, though. It takes time and effort to figure out which school will best suit your needs.

Here's what you can do to get the ball rolling: write down all the schools that are on your mind right now. As you read through this chapter and research schools, write all over this list, adding and scratching off schools and making detailed notes. For starters, you'll need to assess yourself.

ASSESS YOURSELF

Honest self-assessment is not easy. Most of us find it hard to be objective about ourselves, but honesty is essential during the process of selecting a college. You shouldn't underestimate how unpleasant it could be to live, work, and play in an uncomfortable environment. There are several factors to consider when you're assessing yourself.

ACADEMIC INTERESTS

First, consider what major you might want to pursue. Now, don't panic. If you don't know yet what your major will be—even if you have no clue—don't sweat it. Many students aren't sure what they'll major in when they enter college, and most change their major at least once or twice during their college career.

Consider what subjects you like in school, as well as what topics or activities interest you in general; these may relate to a major that you never knew existed. If you were interested in childcare, maybe you'd enjoy studying elementary education, special education, child development, or developmental psychology. An interest in African American studies could lead to related courses in American history, sociology, philosophy, peace studies, or art history. That art history course could spark an interest in architecture, leading to an interest in sculpture, and so on.

You'll be exposed to a whole new range of possibilities in college, so be open to them. But if you already know what major you'd like to pursue, don't make the mistake of attending a college that doesn't even offer it! You can search for majors on www.princetonreview.com and discover which colleges offer yours, and you can find detailed majors profiles in The Princeton Review's *Guide to College Majors*.

SIZE OF STUDENT BODY

Colleges come in all shapes and sizes, and it's your job to figure out which size fits you. The size of the student body is important because it sets the tone for the social environment on campus and the academic environment in the classroom. Exactly how much do schools vary in size? Liberal arts school Marlboro College in Vermont currently enrolls a student body of only 290, while historically black Howard University enrolls around 7,000 students, and Arizona State University enrolls a whopping 35,000 students!

There are advantages and disadvantages at either end of the spectrum. Small schools tend to have smaller classes and are marked by personal instruction from faculty members. If you attend a school with 500 students or less, chances are you'll recognize most faces on campus, and you'll be able to stand out from the crowd pretty easily. At a large school, you'll become acquainted with bigger classes and lectures (sometimes taught by grad students), but the mix of students will probably be more diverse. Large colleges, especially research universities, tend to offer more robust resources for students, along with a wider selection of courses and campus activities.

What type of environment do you see yourself in? Consider whether you would need one-on-one instruction, or would excel at self-motivation and independence.

LOCATION

Would you feel most comfortable attending college near home, or are you looking to get as far from home as possible? Would you like to have the diversions of a major city nearby, or would those be distractions for you? How important is it that you attend college in or around an African American community? How important is it that there are shops, restaurants, and hangouts nearby that cater to your tastes? Issues like these may be very important in determining your happiness and success in college.

You're basically dealing with three types of school settings: urban, suburban, and rural. Each of these has its strengths and weaknesses. The sight, sound, and feel of each can be radically different, so spend some time reflecting on what kind of location suits you best. Don't underestimate the huge impact these factors may have on your college experience. Also, this particular aspect of a college is nearly impossible to evaluate without a proper campus visit.

IS AN HBCU RIGHT FOR YOU?

A school's atmosphere is very important. It determines whether you'll feel comfortable there, whether you'll find your niche. We once heard it put like this: "Going to college ain't about getting in, it's about fitting in." This issue has raised for many African American students the question of whether to attend an Historically Black College or University (HBCU) or a predominantly white institution. African American students can be successful at either; it's up to the student.

Here's the scoop on HBCUs: First of all, by definition, an HBCU is a school that was established before 1964 with the intention of serving the African American community. Often people talk about HBCUs as if they were all the same, but nothing could be further from the truth. There are more than 100 HBCUs in the United States, and they come in all types and sizes. HBCUs can be public or private, and come in both the two-year and four-year variety. Some are large, and some are small. HBCUs are located in twenty states, Washington, D.C., and the Virgin Islands, in both urban and rural areas. Some have competitive admissions standards, whereas others offer quality educational opportunities to students who have less than stellar high school grades. Some, such as Lincoln University of Missouri, actually have large white populations. And few, if any of them, are really all black. (See the back of the book for a list of HBCUs.)

There are some important distinctions in definition to note here: Colleges may be "historically black," "predominantly black," or "having a plurality of black students," and these mean different things. Historically black colleges, as we said above, were established specifically to serve black students, though many white students also attend. Predominantly black colleges have a student population that is more than 50 percent black (so a historically black college could very well also be predominantly black). And in a school that has a plurality of black students, a large segment of the student population is black, though black students do not make up the majority. Only HBCUs have a history of being focused on the African American population.

HBCUs have their advantages and disadvantages. In terms of financial aid, many HBCUs, particularly the smaller private institutions, often lack the resources necessary to offer enough scholarship or grant aid to cover the student's financial needs. This is because most HBCUs do not have large endowments. Some of the better-known predominantly white schools can often provide more generous financial aid packages because they have stronger funding sources. Their funds are often boosted by large donations from alumni and lucrative corporate relationships. In 2002, however, President Bush asked the U.S. Department of Education for a budget increase of $12 million to support programs that enhance HBCUs (as well as Historically Black Graduate Institutions and Hispanic-Serving Institutions), bringing total funding to $350 million. President Bush also requested an additional $264 million in federal support for the African American institutions. Whether these plans are fully accepted or not, they represent a giant step forward in supporting and strengthening these institutions.

The Real World

Some people think that you and every other African American student should attend an HBCU because you will feel more comfortable and perform better if you are surrounded by students from your own culture; others advise that you should not attend an HBCU because it doesn't mirror the "real world" of racial differences that you'll face once you graduate and enter the workforce. We don't agree with either of these schools of thought. Here's why: First of all, some of the larger state universities have more African American students than most HBCUs (a few examples are the University of Maryland, the University of Michigan, Temple University, Wayne State University, and the University of South Carolina). If the goal is simply to "be around" students from your own culture, you can do it at those schools as well as any HBCU. Second, HBCUs reflect the "real world" as well as non-historically black colleges. The fact is, many African American students at non-historically black colleges join all-black fraternities or sororities, form a Black Student Union, and even live in African American dormitories.

The African American environment at *any* college is a factor you should weigh carefully before you apply. Dig beneath the perceptions and stereotypes, and discover for yourself which environment is best for YOU. Visiting the schools you are considering is a great way to assess their environments.

NOW ASSESS THE SCHOOLS . . . AND VISIT!

Now that you have assessed yourself, you can use what you've discovered to reduce the number of colleges to a smaller, more manageable number before you conduct basic research.

Think carefully about the qualities of a school that are important to you. If you are interested in an HBCU in North Carolina with a small student body, in an urban/suburban setting, with a good English program, you might want to consider the following schools: Johnson C. Smith University, Bennett College (women only), Shaw University, North Carolina Central, and Winston-Salem State University. This would be a manageable number of schools to research. Figure out which schools have the most qualities that would make you happy, and eliminate the rest. A systematic approach will ensure that your short-list is a good one.

Now that you have narrowed your choices, let's discuss the factors you should use to assess the colleges. There are *a lot* of factors to consider, even when you know what you're looking for. But you have to start somewhere. We suggest starting with atmosphere, reputation, admissions standards, and cost.

RACIAL ATMOSPHERE ON CAMPUS

At this stage of the process, the on-campus atmosphere for African American students should be a key concern. Ask the tough questions, and make sure you know what you're getting into. Is the college a place where African American students feel comfortable? Do they feel they are succeeding? What percent of African American freshmen return for the sophomore year? How does that percentage compare with the non-African Americans? What has the African American graduation rate been for the past three years? How do these statistics compare with national averages? How do they compare with other colleges you're considering?

Every college keeps track of this information and reports its data to the U.S. Department of Education, so the answers to these questions should be available in the admissions office. If the admissions office doesn't have the answers, then call the public relations office or the office of the president.

There are many ways to gauge the campus vibe at a particular school. Find out whether the African American alumni remain involved with the college after graduation; if so, they probably had a good experience at that college. You can also check out the student newspaper in print or online to read what students are talking about on campus. You can find out what the big issues are, as well as the problems and concerns. In other words, you can hear the real deal from the students' point of view.

Never rely solely on the materials sent to you by colleges. These brochures and booklets are professionally produced and are designed to project the college in the best possible light. Pictures say a lot, but they rarely tell the full story. In fact, in 2000, one major university garnered a heap of controversy over the doctoring of a brochure photo: the face of an African American student was digitally added to a photo of an all-white crowd at a football game. The doctored photo implied that the school was more racially diverse than it actually was when the picture was taken. This is an extreme case, and we don't mean to imply that this type of intentional deception is common. Just be sure to investigate beyond those glossy pages.

Believe Us—You Really Have to Visit the Campus

The best way to learn about a college's atmosphere is to visit the campus. By visiting schools and talking to students (especially African American students and upperclassmen, but not ONLY African American students), you can get a more accurate picture of the school's environment. You can reflect on the size of the student body and campus setting and try to imagine what it would be like to attend each school. Visiting for only a day or staying overnight won't allow you to see everything, but if you ask the right questions and make the right observations, you'll walk away with a wealth of information to help you make your final choice.

There are many ways to approach the college visit. Every college arranges campus tours, but tours may also be offered by local alumni chapters, church or community organizations, or private groups. But whatever you do, don't just follow the tour guide down the beaten path.

Spend some time wandering around to get a better feel for the place. Check out the student union, the cafeteria, sports facilities, and the library. And don't forget the dorms. They may not be palaces, true; but can you see yourself living in them? If not, you may want to investigate the cost and availability of off-campus apartments.

Be sure to interact with students. Ask them how they feel about the school and what they do for fun. Do students hang out on campus most of the time, or is it a suitcase school, where the majority of students go elsewhere for the weekend? Observe how the students act toward each other and toward you—are they friendly and open? Is the student body ethnically and racially diverse?

You'll want to go when the campus is alive, so plan ahead. For additional help planning college visits, including directions and campus highlights, consult *Visiting College Campuses* by Janet Spencer and Sandra Maleson (Random House/The Princeton Review).

THE SCHOOL'S ACADEMIC REPUTATION

Academic reputation can mean different things to different people, so it's sort of a tricky subject. A higher-education professional may have a different view of the matter than a person who does not work at a college or university. For example, medical school admissions officers know that Xavier University in Louisiana is one of the top pre-med programs in the country. And law school admissions committees know that Fisk University in Tennessee has one of the best pre-law programs. People outside of these fields might give you completely different information. Keep in mind that just because a school has a good reputation in one field does not mean it offers strong programs in other disciplines.

What does this mean for you? It means do your research. Read, investigate, and ask questions. Find out what recent graduates are doing now. What percentage was placed in jobs after graduation? What percentage was accepted into graduate programs? Ask what majors are most popular, and ask specifically about the majors you may want to pursue. What have some of the English majors gone on to do? Have any business majors started their own companies? What makes the graduates of this particular college so special?

We Don't Mean "Designer Labels"

When we talk about "academic reputation," we don't mean "name recognition." Harvard and Yale, for example, have an undeniable cachet. But there are hundreds of colleges with less shiny names that will give you a great education! In other words, don't be so label-conscious that you ignore factors that are more important—that is, those personal qualities that may help determine which school is right for you. This isn't to say that name recognition is unimportant. It can play a role when you apply for jobs or graduate school. But don't overrate its importance. Thomas has been reading applications for doctoral programs at Johns Hopkins University for years, and academic reputation does not play as big a role in graduate school admissions as you might think. An "A" student from a nonprestigious college has a much better chance of getting accepted than a "C" student from a prestigious school.

THE COLLEGE'S ADMISSIONS STANDARDS

When making a list of colleges, remember to shoot for the top but also have a backup plan. There's no limit to the number of schools you can apply to, but the application fees really stack up if you've got a long list.

You'll want to select:

- A few schools that are somewhat of an academic "reach," meaning you are uncertain about whether you will be admitted

- A few schools where your academic preparation matches the admissions standards

- At least one school for which your GPA and test scores exceed those of the previous year's freshman class—a "safety school"

The colleges in these categories will be different for every student—your own grades and accomplishments will determine what's a reach and what's a safety.

The basic components of most college applications are your high school transcript, SAT or ACT scores, extracurricular activities, letters of recommendation, essays, and interviews. Assess yourself on these criteria to get an idea of what the admissions officers will think of your application and how you will fare against other applicants. What is your high school GPA? Did you take the tough courses in high school, such as advanced placement (AP) courses? How'd you do on the SAT or ACT? Were you involved in extracurricular activities, and did you hold leadership positions?

The Numbers

Standardized tests are a huge source of stress for many students. Many families spend a lot of money on test prep courses to help their students get the best possible scores. We highly recommend these courses, as well as the many books, computer programs, and practice tests that can help you prepare on your own. High scores on the standardized tests will infinitely strengthen your application and play a big role in how much aid you'll receive; however, when deciding which students to admit, most schools look just as closely at the high school transcript, especially the grades received in college prep courses. We'll say this again and again: The best strategy for getting accepted into the schools you want (and for getting a good financial aid offer) is to take the most challenging courses you can in high school and strive for the best possible grades.

Keep in mind that most college admissions committees do not go strictly by the numbers. They are looking to select well-rounded students with diverse backgrounds and experiences. But keep in mind, too, that it is sometimes difficult to predict what "outside forces" are affecting the admissions process. For example, some state schools are prohibited from admitting too many students from out of state—so it's possible for a student with lower grades and standardized test scores to be admitted over a seemingly more qualified student. When deciding where to apply, consider what the schools are looking for—then do your best to package yourself in a way they can't refuse.

Two-Year Colleges

While this book focuses on four-year colleges, we think it's worthwhile to mention another option: junior and community colleges. These colleges often get a bad rap because many people believe that they provide students with an inferior education. "They" refer to these schools as "the thirteenth grade." But your goals, academic abilities, or financial situation might make a junior or community college an option worth considering.

Junior and community colleges are alike in many ways, and their names are often used interchangeably. Two-year "junior colleges" were developed in the late nineteenth century and were meant to provide the first two years of a student's college education. As they grew in popularity, many junior colleges began calling themselves "community colleges" to appeal to people who might *not* be planning to move into a four-year school. But there are some distinctions between these two types of schools. Typically, the two years students spend in a junior college correspond to the first two years of a four-year school, which makes the transition to a four-year school easy—and transferring is usually the intention of the students who go there. On the other hand, community colleges offer associate degrees and are usually not seen as stepping-stones into four-year programs. Community colleges are generally government-supported and have a wide range of programs that appeal to entire communities.

According to the American Association of Community Colleges (on the association's website, www.aacc.nche.edu, the terms "junior college" and "community college" are treated as synonyms), four out of ten college grads started at a junior college. We found some other eye-opening facts from the *National Profiles of Community Colleges: Trends and Statistics*:

- Junior colleges enroll 44 percent of all U.S. under-graduates.

- Junior colleges enroll 45 percent of first-time freshmen.

- 46 percent of black undergraduate students are enrolled in junior colleges.

- 32.8 percent of students receive financial aid.

- The average annual tuition is $1,518.

Most junior colleges are open to everyone and have no selection criteria. The classes are much smaller than those at many colleges and universities. Professors are usually retired professionals or experienced people who are working in their fields of expertise. While junior colleges are inexpensive compared to four-year colleges, they still offer financial aid packages.

If funds are especially tight, you can spend one or two years at a junior college and earn an associate's degree, then transfer to a four-year school. In fact, many junior colleges are "feeder schools" for their state's four-year institutions, and earning an associate's degree means automatic acceptance to the four-year school. A little-known fact is that many students who now attend major state schools actually saved money by taking their basic courses at the local junior college, then transferring the credits over.

Of course, choosing this option means potentially altering your idea of what the college experience means for you; community colleges are almost always commuter schools, and the "college life" you've probably heard so much about usually doesn't exist to a great extent on these campuses. Still, we want you to be aware of every possible option.

THE COST

You bought this book because you're worried about the cost of college—and hey, who isn't? It might be tempting to look at college price tags and simply select the "cheapest" schools. After all, a "cheap" college isn't necessarily a "bad" college. But if you automatically rule out schools that are expensive, you're making a big mistake. Why? Because of a very important concept called **expected family contribution,** or **EFC**—the amount of money that the federal government determines you should be able to contribute to the college bill. Theoretically, this amount remains the same whether that bill is high or low. (We'll go into greater detail on your EFC in Step 3.)

If an expensive college really wants you, the financial aid package you are offered will usually be generous. The most expensive, selective private schools generally have the largest endowments and, therefore, are in the best position to offer aid to students.

As we said in Step 1, both students and parents should be fully aware of the investments you're about to make. Don't go into this blindly—but don't let the price tags discourage you, either.

SUMMING UP

Deciding where you will spend the next four or five years of your life is a major decision—one of the most important decisions you'll make. Weigh your options carefully. Consider your individual needs and factor in the cost appropriately. High price does not always equal high quality, and vice versa. There are plenty of schools that offer a great education at a low cost.

Most important, choose a school for the *right reasons.* When you watch the next March Madness NCAA basketball tournament on TV, don't get carried away by the winning team. You wouldn't want to make your most important academic decision based solely on who wins the big game.

STEP 3: GET YOUR HEAD AROUND FINANCIAL AID

Applying for financial aid really isn't as complicated as it might seem. The big words, jargon, and acronyms financial aid pros use can make the process seem confusing, but we'll help you sort it out.

First, let's work on tossing out some of the ideas that *they* may have put in your head.

FINANCIAL AID MYTHS

MYTH #1: IF YOU HAVE A HIGH-PAYING JOB, YOU CAN'T GET FINANCIAL AID

Many people mistakenly assume that they will not qualify for aid because they make too much money. To qualify for federal financial aid, you must:

- Be a U.S. citizen or eligible noncitizen with a valid Social Security number

- Have a high school diploma or a General Education Development (GED) certificate, or pass an approved ability-to-benefit (ATB) test

- Enroll in an eligible program as a regular student working toward a degree or certificate

- Register (or have registered) with the Selective Service if you are a male between the ages of 18 and 25

Financial aid can be based on "need" or "merit." Basically, the less money you have, the more need-based aid you will qualify for. Merit-based aid refers to funds awarded for academic performance, leadership, volunteerism, or some other characteristic.

In 1999–2000, 55 percent of undergraduates received financial aid of some kind or another, and African American students received more federal aid than other students. Students from well-off families may receive *less* aid than needy families, but you should never assume that you aren't eligible for financial aid.

MYTH #2: YOU SHOULDN'T EVEN APPLY TO A SCHOOL YOU CAN'T AFFORD

This is a common misconception. Remember what we told you in Step 2? Regardless of how much a school costs, your expected family contribution—the amount of money you are deemed able to pay—should remain the same. In other words, theoretically, you won't pay more for an expensive school than you will for an inexpensive one. Cost shouldn't be the main criteria in your college search, but you should apply to a financial safety school, just in case.

MYTH #3: I'M A PARENT, AND AFTER MY SAVINGS ARE CONSIDERED FOR FINANCIAL AID, I'LL HAVE NOTHING LEFT!

Not true. While the federal processors will look at all of your savings, they will assess your assets at a rate of only 5.65 percent, and your income at 47 percent. We'll talk more about this in Step 4.

Myth #4: You Don't Have to File with the Government; There's Enough Money Available from Local Organizations

Although we definitely encourage you to investigate sources of scholarships and grants in your local community, believing that you can pay for college this way is a mistake. When you consider the many thousands of dollars that college will cost, you can see that finding this much money would be a feat to behold. Federal loan programs are meant to help you, and with interest rates as low as they are, you should take advantage of them by filing your government forms. Don't realize too late that the "free money" from local organizations and random scholarships that seemed so promising is harder to find than you'd expected.

Myth #5: Financial Aid Depends on Grades

This is neither entirely true nor entirely false. Each college wants the best possible class of students. If a student has a stellar high school record, colleges will likely be more eager to persuade him or her to choose their school, and may give more financial aid as an incentive. However, the basis of financial aid is the EFC, which measures the family's financial situation. Your income and assets will be the same whether your child has straight A's or not; scholarships, though, are often awarded on the basis of merit.

WHO DECIDES HOW MUCH I CAN PAY FOR COLLEGE?

Once you fill out the Free Application for Federal Student Aid (FAFSA) form (more on this later) and any other required forms, such as the CSS/Financial Aid PROFILE, you'll send it to the federal processor—the agency that determines the amount students and parents can pay for college. The federal processor crunches your numbers and then sends the information to you in a document called the **Student Aid Report (SAR).** The SAR is also sent to the schools you are applying to, which you listed on the form initially. Check the SAR to make sure all information has been processed correctly, then put it in a safe place—it's an important document, and you'll have to refer back to it later. Now you are in the hands of the **Financial Aid Officer (FAO)** at each of these schools. Most schools employ a handful of FAOs, and one of them will be assigned to you.

Your FAO reviews the report from the federal processor and interviews you (the student). The FAO has the flexibility to make final decisions about your aid package. Factors such as whether the college uses the federal or institutional methodology, how badly the school wants the student, and how much scholarship money is available at the school help the FAO to determine whether the federal processor's figure will appear in the school's financial aid offer—or whether you'll be paying more or less than that amount to attend.

About a month after receiving the SAR report, you will receive a financial aid offer in the mail from the schools you applied to.

Federal and Institutional Methodology

There are two methods used to determine your EFC. The **federal methodology** is the method that is used by the government and by public institutions. The **institutional methodology** is an alternate method typically used by private schools that are testing students' eligibility for scholarships and grants under their direct control. Schools that use the institutional methodology must use the federal methodology to determine the amount of federally funded scholarships or grants (such as the Pell Grant) they will give students. Federal money that filters through the school, though, as is the case with work-study, may be subject to the institutional methodology.

The institutional methodology requires you to fill out an additional document called the **PROFILE** form, which is processed by the College Board (www.collegeboard.com). Note also that many public and private colleges and scholarship programs use information collected on the PROFILE form to help them award nonfederal student aid. Different schools may require other forms that are similar to the PROFILE form and will be provided by the schools.

Regardless of what the forms are called, they are designed to gather the same basic financial information: parents' income and assets, and students' income and assets. They match your financial information against the basic costs of going to college: tuition and fees, room and board, books and supplies, and travel and personal expenses.

The federal and institutional methodologies are quite different, as they have different guidelines for calculating income, expenses, assets, liabilities, and students' income and assets. For more on these differences, you may wish to consult *Paying for College Without Going Broke*, by Kalman A. Chany with Geoff Martz (Random House/The Princeton Review).

YOUR EFC AND THE BASE INCOME YEAR

Whether you've been preparing for college for many years or you've just begun thinking about college in the student's senior year of high school, the process formally starts at the same time. The tax year before the student enrolls in college is the year that will be analyzed to determine your family's aid eligibility. This is called the base income year, and it's a crucial period because it sets the tone for the types of financial aid packages you can expect throughout the college years (though you will have to reapply every year). Your assets and income from the base year are used to calculate how much aid you are eligible for, so we highly recommend that you reduce your taxable income as much as possible during the base income year. The less income you receive, the more financial aid you can qualify for. We will offer some tips on this in Step 4.

The purpose of these forms is to provide the federal processor with enough financial information to decide how much students and parents can fork up for college. Schools want to know how much money they can count on you to contribute before they decide how much aid to give. As we mentioned earlier, the amount the federal processors determine you can afford to pay is called the EFC. The difference between this amount and the cost of the school is called your **need.** The purpose of financial aid is to cover your need. In some cases, a school won't cover your entire need and you are left with **unmet need.**

The relationship between college cost, EFC, need, and unmet need is displayed in Figure 3.1.

Figure 3.1 Need, Unmet Need, and EFC

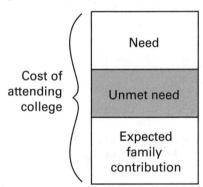

How Is EFC Determined?

Every student who wishes to receive any financial aid must fill out the **Free Application for Federal Student Aid (FAFSA).** Based on the information you provide on the FAFSA, a federal processor uses a fairly complicated formula that takes into account a number of factors. The federal processor comes up with a figure for the expected student contribution and the expected parent contribution and adds them together to come up with the grand total—the expected family contribution. The formula does not consider the cost of any individual college, so regardless of whether the school's tuition if $5,000 or $20,000, your EFC will be about the same. (Schools using the institutional methodology may have a somewhat different figure.) The factors considered in the EFC formula are:

- Parents' income and student's income

- Parents' and students' accumulated savings, investments, and other assets

- The amount of taxes paid

- Family size and the number of children simultaneously enrolled in college

- The age of the older parent and how close they may be to retirement

- The student's own financial resources

Figure 3.2 Why the Cost of College Should Not Be Your First Consideration

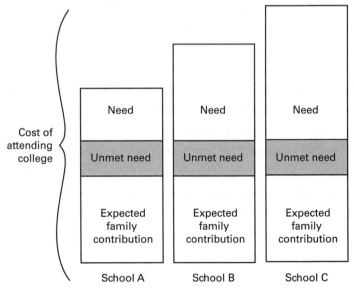

Here's a breakdown of how each factor can impact your EFC:

Family Income

This figure includes the student's income from work, parents' income from work, untaxed income, and **adjusted gross income (AGI).** The contributions you make to your 401(k) or other tax-deferred retirement plans, as well as child support and other Social Security payments are also considered income. In general, the higher your family income, the higher your EFC will be. Check out the following examples from the U.S. Department of Education to get an idea of what your estimated EFC might be depending on your income range. This is strictly an estimate—these figures do not take into consideration any other factors that are used to determine EFC. Your EFC could be higher or lower than the estimate shown for your salary range.

Expected Family Contribution (EFC)

Family income level	Typical EFC range
Below $20,000	$0 – $800
$20,000 – $40,000	$900 – $3,400
$40,000 – $60,000	$4,100 – $7,650
$60,000 – $80,000	$8,950 – $12,850
$80,000 – $100,000	$12,000 – $16,850
Above $100,000	$17,800 – $33,800

National Center for Education Statistics, National
Postsecondary Student Aid Study, 1995–1996

Savings, Investments, Assets, and Liabilities

Families are expected to tap into all available resources to pay for the student's education. The federal processor will consider the parents' and student's **assets,** which include stocks, property (other than your home), cash, checking accounts, savings accounts, educational IRAs, mutual funds, money market accounts, certificates of deposit (CDs), U.S. savings bonds, and trusts. The more assets you have, the more money you can contribute to college costs.

The value of your home is not included in the federal aid formula, but if you're applying to any private schools, you'll have to submit this information on the PROFILE form. The value of your car is not included in your assets in either case, as it turns into a depreciating asset the moment you drive it out of the dealership parking lot.

Liabilities are the debts you owe to various lenders that ultimately detract from the value of your assets. Debts against the specific assets listed above will be subtracted from your available assets in the aid formula, but the following debts are not considered: unsecured loans, personal loans, educational loans, auto loans, or credit card balances or other forms of consumer debt. You'll want to minimize these debts during the base income year by paying off some of your debts.

Taxes Paid

Here's one of the cases where paying a lot of taxes is a good thing. Federal taxes are considered to be an expense, helping to offset your income. A higher tax bill can help lower your EFC.

Children

Those little people who have been giving you joys as well as financial pains over the years can really pay off for you here. Under the institutional method, families can receive credit for additional school tuition, such as your college student's younger siblings who are in a private elementary school. The more children in your family, the lower your EFC will be per child, especially if there are two or more children who will be in college at the same time.

Age of Older Parent

The federal processor recognizes that as adults get closer to their retirement years, their assets need to be protected. The formula accounts for this by considering less of the parents' assets based on how close the oldest parent is to age sixty-five. The following table, with figures from the Federal Register, shows how assets are protected according to age.

Oldest Parent's Age	Amount of Assets Protected (When There are 2 Parents)	Amount of Assets Protected (When There is 1 Parent)
30	$11,400	$5,600
40	$34,300	$16,700
50	$44,000	$20,800
60	$58,300	$26,600
61	$60,000	$27,400
62	$62,000	$28,100
63	$63,800	$28,900
64	$66,000	$29,700
65 or older	$68,200	$30,700

Source: Federal Register

Student's Own Finances

Both the federal and institutional methods consider the student's income and assets but do so in different ways. Under the federal methodology, there is no minimum contribution expected from a freshman student. The first $2,250 (after taxes) the student earns is excluded from consideration, but once the earnings exceed about $2,436, additional earnings will be assessed as income at 50 percent and as an asset (if the money is saved) at 35 percent.

Under the institutional methodology, students are expected to contribute at least $1,150, regardless of whether they've ever worked a day in their lives. Once a student's income exceeds $2,490, he or she will have to pay up to seventy-five cents per additional dollar earned. The more income and assets the student has, the higher the EFC will likely be.

CALCULATE YOUR OWN EFC

Worksheets that help you calculate your own EFC are usually lengthy and can be somewhat confusing. As an alternative, www.PrincetonReview.com offers a calculator that does the computations for you. Just gather your financial paperwork, type in the appropriate information, and—poof!—your estimated EFC appears! Each question has its own detailed explanation, in case there is any confusion. The number will be an *estimate*, but it will give you an idea of what you can expect your contribution to be.

WHERE DOES THE MONEY COME FROM?

There are five basic sources of college funding:

1. Federal government

2. State government

3. Private sources such as civic groups, unions, corporations, churches and other organizations, and private lenders

4. University-based aid

5. Personal (family) resources

The federal government is the largest provider of college financial aid. There is some aid available for nearly everyone, but naturally your financial situation will play the biggest role in how much and what type of aid you can get.

The financial aid package you receive will consist of a combination of the following:

- Grants

- Scholarships

- Federal work-study

- Student loans (subsidized Stafford loans and Federal Perkins loans)

GRANTS

Grants = free money, never to be refused. Here's a breakdown of the different grants you may encounter:

Federal Grants

We're talking about need-based, tax-free money that you don't have to pay back.

The Federal Pell Grant

This grant money is usually reserved for low-income families. You may receive up to $4,000 per year if you qualify.

The Federal Supplemental Education Opportunity Grant (SEOG)

The federal government gives each school a certain amount of money to distribute to students as the college sees fit. This award can range from $100 to $4,000.

State Grants

This money is typically given by the state to students applying to schools in their home state; sometimes, students applying to schools in nearby states that have reciprocal agreements with their home state may also receive state grants. These grants are based on need but may take into account the tuition price of each particular school.

School Grants

Each college makes up its own rules for awarding institutional grants. Some schools offer this money based purely on need, while others offer merit-based grant money as well. The likelihood that a student will receive grant money from a school will depend on the size of that particular school's endowment.

SCHOLARSHIPS

Scholarships are another form of free money—but sometimes there's a catch. Read the fine print.

School Scholarships

Traditionally, schools award scholarships based on academic, artistic, or athletic merit. Some schools, however, take need into consideration as well.

There are two things you need to ask about a scholarship offered to you by a college:

1. Does this scholarship go toward my need, or will it be used to reduce my expected family contribution?

   (The answer will likely be the former—institutional scholarships generally count toward fulfilling your need.)

2. What are the conditions of the scholarship?

   (There may be a certain GPA you need to maintain in order to hold onto an academic scholarship, for example.)

If the school doesn't offer you any scholarships, ask what scholarships are available and what criteria students must meet to qualify.

Outside Scholarships

A student may be able to win scholarship money from a variety of private sources, such as civic groups, unions, corporations, churches, and other organizations. You may be eligible to receive scholarship money from the company your mother works for, or you may be eligible because you have asthma! You'll be amazed at all the scholarship opportunities that are out there once you start looking.

Don't expect them to be easy money, though. Most scholarship applications require basic information about you and your academic standing, as well as an essay or supplemental material. And these scholarships operate on their own schedules, so you'll have to be sure to keep every single deadline in mind. Although there seems to be a lot of free money out there, beware: Often, the amounts don't add up to a huge sum. Of course, any amount of aid is helpful and should be accepted gracefully, but don't rely on these scholarships to pay the bill.

Here is a very specific reason why you *can't* rely on scholarships to pay your way: They often go toward your need, rather than your EFC. You are required to inform each college about outside scholarship money. Often, (and always, if you inform the colleges before your award letter is sent) the schools will sweep the scholarship right into your need, replacing grant money. Some scholarship sources inform the schools directly; others leave it up to you. If you hold out on telling colleges about this outside aid until it's time to negotiate the package, there's a chance that they'll allow a portion of the scholarship to cover your EFC or replace some loan money in the aid offer. (Read more on scholarships in Step 4.)

Federal Work-Study

This program gives students the opportunity to obtain part-time jobs through the college; the jobs are usually on campus and pay the minimum wage or higher. Because the federal government pays a portion of federal work-study wages, and because the amount the government is willing to pay is the amount of your work-study award, *your work-study earnings cannot exceed the amount of your work-study award.* This means that you'll have a limited number of hours that you'll be permitted to work. The job possibilities are varied, from serving food in the cafeteria to working in an administrative office. Wages from work-study jobs are exempt from the financial aid formulas.

One of Will's work-study jobs included raising the American flag each morning and lowering and properly folding it each evening before dusk. He also received work-study funds for being the managing editor of the college's student newspaper. Work-study can lead to bigger and better things, too.

The Skinny on Loans

Loans are money you borrow that you will have to pay back with interest. Some loan programs are for students, and others are for parents. The maximum loan amount you can get will depend on your year in school and the cost of the school you attend.

There are basically two types of loans you'll encounter on your financial aid journey: **need-based,** which go toward meeting your remaining need, and **non-need-based,** which go toward helping to pay your EFC.

The following loans are need-based and may appear in your financial aid offer: Federal Perkins loans, subsidized Federal Stafford loans, state loans, and college loans.

The following are not need-based and should *not* appear in your award letter: unsubsidized federal Stafford loans, PLUS loans, and other alternative loans. They are intended to help you pay your EFC.

Federal Perkins loans (formerly National Direct Student Loans) and Stafford loans are the best need-based loans because their interest rates are very reasonable—far below typical consumer loan rates. We recommend that the student accept these loans if they are offered in the award letter.

Federal Perkins Loans

Federal Perkins loans are great because they are **subsidized**— meaning, interest does not accrue until six months after you graduate, leave college, or drop below part-time status, which is also when you begin making loan payments. The federal government distributes Perkins loan funds to colleges, which, in turn, assign the money to the neediest students. The FAOs then determine how much you will receive; $4,000 is the limit for each year of study, and $20,000 is the maximum total amount that can be borrowed. In 2001, the average Perkins loan awarded was $1,681. Students can take out the loan with a parent cosigning and must sign a promissory note that certifies their commitment to loan repayment. The current interest rate on Perkins loans is 5 percent.

Federal Stafford Loans

Stafford loans come in two varieties: subsidized and unsubsidized. The subsidized Stafford loan, like the Perkins loan, does not accrue interest while you are in school. **Unsubsidized** Stafford loans, on the other hand, begin accruing interest as soon as the loan is disbursed (when the lender pays the school the full loan amount). It will continue to accrue interest until paid in full.

If you have an unsubsidized Stafford loan, you can choose to make interest payments while you are in school, or you can allow the interest to accumulate while you're in school or during other periods of nonpayment. If you do this, the loan will be **capitalized.** This means that the interest will be added to the principal (the sum of money owed) of your loan, and interest will accrue based on this growing principal amount. In other words, you'll be paying interest on the interest from the loan—you'll be paying back much more than you should have to. We don't have to tell you that this should be avoided, if at all possible!

Subsidized Stafford loans are need-based and count toward your need; unsubsidized Stafford loans are not need-based and are used to help pay your EFC. Under both loan programs, the amount of money a student can borrow increases each year of college. This nearly guarantees that a student with Stafford loans will have a shifting package, where loan money will replace more grant money each year. For dependent students, the maximum loan amounts are $2,625 for freshman year; $3,500 for sophomore year; and $5,500 for junior and senior year. Independent students may borrow up to $6,625 for freshman year; $7,500 for sophomore year; and $10,500 for each remaining year (a portion of the loans for independent students must be unsubsidized).

In 1999–2000, 96 percent of undergrads with loans took out Stafford loans, and the average loan amount was $4,500.

State Loans

The terms of state loans vary from state to state and should be researched with that in mind. Some state loans are for students, others are for parents, and often, they are available to both residents and nonresidents attending college in that state. (Check out our directory of state financial aid offices at the back of the book.)

College Loans

These loans, too, vary greatly, so read the fine print of each offer, and make sure you catch the interest rate. Some unappealing college loans have very high interest rates and must be repaid almost immediately upon graduation.

PLUS Loans

Federal Parent Loans for Undergraduate Students (PLUS loans) are for parents. Even though PLUS loans are not need-based, you'll need to pass a credit check to be given the green light. If you have bad credit, you might still be able to get a PLUS loan with a cosigner. In 1999–2000, 6 percent of parents took out PLUS loans, averaging $7,100 per loan.

Alternative Loans

If all else fails, you can turn to educational loans, offered by banks, credit unions, and private lending companies. You'll have to do some research comparing offers, but you'll find that many of these private loans have competitive interest rates. When researching loans, make sure you ask about the interest rate (how much? fixed or variable?), repayment options, and extra fees, and find out who the borrower will be (parent or student?) and whether a cosigner is necessary. Visit www.princetonreview.com/college/finance/finLoans.asp to check out The Princeton Review's selected lenders.

CONCLUSION

They say the college years are the best of your life. And in this case, usually *they* are right. Everyone deserves a college education—no matter how rich or poor the person is. We hope one thing you take away from this book is the confidence to go after the schools you love, with the knowledge that money is out there to help you pay the bill. If you've taken this information to heart, you're ready to go after the financial aid you deserve. Good luck.

STEP 4: LEARN HOW TO GET THE FINANCIAL AID YOU NEED AND DESERVE

ANOTHER WORD ABOUT COST

As our sons have been following the path to choosing the right college, they haven't thought much about what it costs to attend any of them. They've looked at schools ranging from historically black colleges to predominantly white institutions. Large universities, small colleges, and in-state and out-of-state schools have been on their lists. Campus visits? Done that. Researched each school thoroughly? Check that one off too.

They've read magazines such as *Black Voices Quarterly* (also known as BVQ), which covers the campus lifestyle at HBCUs, and *Black Enterprise*, which, in partnership with DayStar Research, offers a biennial ranking of the top fifty colleges for African Americans. But ask them about the costs of attending each of the schools and they give you a blank look and a shrug. And actually, this is okay. As we said before, families should discuss college selections together—students should be as much aware of the price tags as parents are—but our sons had the right idea about focusing more on the unique academic, cultural, and personal qualities of each school than the cost. As we mentioned in Step 2, the school with the lowest price tag isn't always the most affordable.

THE MOST IMPORTANT TIP

In order to qualify for financial aid, your goal should be to appear as "needy" as possible without lying. As we pointed out in Step 1, sometimes we African Americans tend to focus on the "top line." But when it comes to qualifying for financial aid, your top line can hurt you. The smaller your taxable income is, the better. Remember: the goal here is not to focus on how much money you make, but on how much you get to keep.

The parents' tax return is the key document that FAOs pay attention to. The information on the financial aid forms must match up with the information on the tax return. If not, the red flags will go up, jeopardizing your chances of getting aid. For this reason, you may want to consider filling out your tax returns and financial aid forms at the same time. Doing this will allow you to take advantage of some of the following financial aid tips before your numbers are set in stone on the tax forms.

HOW TO LOWER YOUR EFC AND GET MORE AID

There are a few strategies you can employ to get the lowest EFC possible before you even fill out the FAFSA. In Step 3, we explained the key factors the EFC formula considers. Now we'll share some thoughts on how you can tweak those factors to reduce the EFC. If your student is more than five years away from entering college, you can be very proactive and get a strong handle on your financial situation. If your student is entering college next year or this fall, you're behind—but you can still get aggressive and save yourself some money.

To help you before you fill out the FAFSA, we'll offer some long- and short-term strategies to deal with your income and assets according to the aid formulas. Here's a quick reminder before we begin: **Income** is the money you earned or received over the past year, both taxable and untaxed. It includes your salary, alimony, unemployment benefits, child support, deferred compensation, dividends, and interest. **Assets** include stocks, property (other than your home), cash, checking accounts, savings accounts, educational IRAs, mutual funds, money market accounts, CDs, U.S. savings bonds, and trusts. Parents' assets are assessed at a maximum rate of 5.65 percent, while student's assets are assessed at 35 percent under the federal methodology and 25 percent under the institutional methodology.

LONG-TERM STRATEGIES FOR THOSE WITH TIME BEFORE THE COLLEGE BILL HITS

- Because the base income year (the tax year before your student enters college) is farther off, parents should keep making as much money as they can. We know it may seem as if having less money is to your advantage, but more money is always a good thing. Regardless of your income, you may still qualify for aid because income is only one factor that's considered. Many experts predict that the cost of both public and private colleges will increase at a rate of about 5 percent per year, so be prepared. Save, manage your money wisely, and invest with the help of a financial planner.

- If you've been thinking about starting a business, waiting until a year or two before your child starts college would be a smart move. Businesses are often unprofitable in the first few years, so you may have a base income year with high start-up costs (detracting from your assets) and low sales (reducing your income); business assets are also assessed at a much lower rate than are personal assets. And if all goes well, business will pick up once the company has carved out its place in the market. You'll be golden as far as the federal aid is concerned; the institutional methodology, however, doesn't count your business losses when calculating your eligibility.

Be careful when choosing this strategy: IRS auditors and FAOs are hip to "dummy businesses," so make sure your business is legitimate. This is a rather risky tactic, so you should consult your accountant or a financial planner before going ahead with this plan.

- Because time is on your side, you can take advantage of the benefits of compounding interest. If you consistently save money each month, over a period of years it will grow tremendously. A mutual fund is a good savings vehicle for a high return. Your investment portfolio should be diversified to minimize risk. The younger the child, the more money you should have in aggressive growth funds; as the student gets closer to high school graduation, you should shift to less risky investments. A financial planner can help you figure out your options.

- A word of caution: Don't put savings or other assets in the student's name. Putting assets in a child's name may be good for tax purposes, but not for financial aid planning. As we said, the student's assets are assessed at a 35 percent rate, whereas assets in the parent's name are assessed at only 5.6 percent. Putting assets in a child's name is one of the worst financial aid mistakes you can make.

- Some families also choose to invest in state-run savings plans that are specifically for education. We do not recommend that you use these plans unless you are absolutely sure you won't qualify for aid. These funds will count as assets or resources that decrease your eligibility for aid. Examples of these educational plans are Section 529 prepaid tuition plans and education IRAs.

SHORT-TERM STRATEGIES IF COLLEGE IS JUST AROUND THE CORNER

- It would be difficult for most working people to reduce their annual salary. And why would anyone want to, when more money is always needed to keep up with inflation? If you receive an annual bonus, though, you can ask your employer to defer it into a non–base income year. The bonus will be included in your assets instead of counting twice—as assets *and* income.

- Adjust your income tax withholding so that when you file your return, instead of getting a huge refund, you end up paying exactly or close to the exact amount you were supposed to pay. When you receive a refund, it actually means that you overpaid your taxes and allowed the government to use your income interest-free for investing. By adjusting your withholding, you should have more money available each pay period to go toward savings and investing. Visit www.irs.gov and use the calculator to estimate your withholding based on your salary.

- If you worked a lot of overtime or received retroactive pay, ask to have the payments applied to a non–base income year. Remember: you want the base income year to reflect typical earnings. If this is not possible, go ahead and take the additional pay, then write to the FAO of each school your student is applying to and tell them that you won't get this extra money every year. Unless you explain this, the FAO will assume this amount is your expected annual salary and will adjust your financial aid package accordingly. Include your tax return from the year prior to the base income year as an example of typical wages.

- Consider starting a business. (See long-term strategies.)

- Fill out the short forms or don't file at all (if the IRS allows). Parents will have an automatic EFC of zero dollars if they have a combined adjusted gross income or combined income from work of $13,000 or less, and if they can file the 1040A or 1040EZ, or are not required to file. Families can have their assets excluded from the federal aid formulas if they meet the

Simplified Needs test. To qualify, parents must have combined adjusted gross income below $50,000, income from work below $50,000, and each family member must file the 1040A or 1040EZ, or not file at all.

- Focus on the base income year. If you are planning to make big purchases such as a car, do it now and pay cash. Take the money out of your savings. This will reduce the appearance of your cash assets.

- During this year, don't use any flexible spending plans offered by your employer. Remember that having a higher-than-usual tax bill helps you get more financial aid.

- Pay off your credit card bills and use cash. This will reduce your assets, because the aid formulas are blind to credit card debt, and increase your aid.

HOW CAN THE STUDENT HELP?

There are actually quite a few things that students can do to maximize aid eligibility and help defray the costs of college.

TAKE COLLEGE-LEVEL CLASSES WHILE YOU'RE IN HIGH SCHOOL

Some courses directly translate into subject-specific introductory credits that are accepted at many colleges. Advanced placement (AP) classes can earn you college credit too, but credit is contingent upon your score on the corresponding AP exam. The test costs around seventy-five dollars but can save you several hundred dollars: If you score a minimum of 3 out of 5 (although 4 out of 5 greatly improves your chances), you might not have to take an introductory course in that subject.

Start Elsewhere and Transfer in Later

If your top-choice school is very expensive, consider beginning at a junior college or at a four-year school that costs less than your EFC amount. After two years, you can transfer to the more expensive college (assuming, of course, you've performed well enough academically to be accepted). After you graduate, the total bill will be much less than it would have been if you'd gone to the expensive school as a freshman. Meanwhile, you'll earn your bachelor's degree from your first-choice school. This transfer tactic is also used by students who were not initially accepted at their first-choice school.

Transferring isn't always easy—college is about more than classes, after all—but it's an option that can save you money.

Ever Imagine Yourself Wearing Fatigues?

There are a few military options you may want to consider. The Reserve Officers' Training Corps (ROTC) program is offered by each branch of the military. Participation requires a few hours of your time per week and an intense summer training program between junior and senior years, but the rewards are great: up to $17,000 per year toward tuition and fees, not to mention a book allowance and additional subsistence allowance. When you graduate as an Army ROTC cadet, you'll be commissioned as a second lieutenant in the army, and your required service time will vary depending on the scholarship amount you received.

You may also choose to commit one weekend per month and two weeks per year to the National Guard in return for up to $263 a month while you're enrolled in college and up to 75 percent of tuition costs not covered by the G.I. Bill.

TRY COMMUNITY SERVICE

AmeriCorps offers a wide array of service opportunities for students, who may cater their volunteer work to career goals. AmeriCorps volunteers are awarded an education voucher for $4,725 that can be used to pay for tuition or pay back student loans. To earn this voucher, you must serve a ten- to twelve-month full-time tour of duty; you may also choose to serve part-time for a reduced education voucher. (Make sure this service grant is used toward your EFC and *not* your need, as it was in some cases where students served prior to college.) For more information, visit www.americorps.org.

Generally speaking, involvement in volunteer work will open up a range of service-related scholarship possibilities; on the extreme tip of these opportunities, students pursuing a career in health care may receive a scholarship through the National Health Service Corps that covers tuition and fees (tax free) and includes a monthly stipend. Following graduation, scholarship recipients work in underprivileged communities, caring for residents' health for one year per year of scholarship coverage, with a two-year minimum service requirement. For more information, visit http://nhsc.bhpr.hrsa.gov/about/.

There are also some other service organizations that offer sizeable monetary rewards, such as Head Start, Peace Corps, and VISTA, whose volunteers may be relieved of some of their federal loan obligations.

CHECK OUT SCHOOLS WITH FREE TUITION

Did you know that there are actually a number of schools in the United States whose students attend free of charge? They include the military academies (West Point, Naval, Coast Guard, Air Force, and Merchant Marine); specialty schools Webb Institute in Long Island (marine engineering and naval architecture), Cooper Union in New York City (art, architecture, and engineering), and tiny Deep Springs College in Nevada ("service and idealism"); and schools that require a mere ten to fifteen hours of work per week in exchange for free attendance, such as College of the Ozarks in Missouri and Berea College in Kentucky.

CONSIDER COOPERATIVE EDUCATION

You also have the option of earning money to pay for tuition while gaining valuable work experience through cooperative education. Students participating in this program often alternate semesters between full-time enrollment and full-time employment and may take around five years to graduate, but those extra resume bullet points put these students at an advantage over their peers in the job market. If you are interested in learning more about cooperative education, contact your prospective schools about how it would affect your aid package, and visit the National Commission for Cooperative Education at www.co-op.edu.

APPLY FOR SCHOLARSHIPS

You are part of an underrepresented group (that includes anyone who is economically, racially, ethnically, geographically, or socially different from the majority of the applicant pool), and there are a large number of scholarships designed specifically for African American students. You should contact the schools you're interested in to see if any such scholarships are available. There's no need to limit yourself to just these scholarships, though. Apply for those that are not race-specific as well.

As we mentioned in Step 3, you are required to tell colleges about any money you are awarded from outside sources, and that money is generally used to compensate for your need, *not* your EFC. You can try to convince the FAOs to count a portion of your scholarship toward your need, but don't count on it working out in your favor; on the other hand, if you end up having any unmet need, scholarships are a great way to bridge that gap.

So how do you search for scholarships? Talk to your high school guidance counselor, contact the financial aid office, search for scholarships online, visit your local library, and just ask around. Your house of worship, neighborhood group, local government, and corporations are also great sources of scholarship information. Organizations such as United Negro College Fund (UNCF), the Thurgood Marshall Scholarship Fund, National Association for Equal Opportunity (NAFEO), The Urban League, National Association for the Advancement of Colored People (NAACP), 100 Black Men of America, as well as Black Greek letter fraternities and sororities all offer various types of scholarships geared toward African American students. Some are based on merit, requiring academic excellence, while others are based on need.

There are a couple of things you'll want to keep in mind when searching and applying for scholarships. First, each private scholarship may have its own deadline, so make sure you keep track of your financial aid schedule. Give yourself time to fill out the application and write an essay, if it is required, well before that date. Second, beware of scholarship scams. If a scholarship asks for money or your credit number, or claims you won some contest that you never entered, it's probably not legit.

There are quite a few services that can match you with scholarship sources based on the criteria you are looking for in a school, such as cost and location, or your own characteristics, like ethnic background. We have listed a few sites here to get you started.

Internet Resources for Private Scholarships

www.princetonreview.com/college/finance/articles/ scholarships/scholarsearch.asp

www.nul.org/scholarships.html

www.uncf.org

www.gmsp.org

www.ronbrown.org

www.finaid.org

www.ed.gov/offices/OSFAP/Students/

www.scholarships.com

www.absolutelyscholarships.com

STEP 5: APPLY FOR AID

Okay. Now you're ready to get down to the business of applying for financial aid. By now you should have a better idea of what financial aid is all about and how you can best work the system. It's time to put your plan into action.

Let's start with an overview of the basics. In order to qualify for financial aid, it is your responsibility to obtain all necessary forms and file them accurately and on time. After the forms have been sent to the federal processor at the need-analysis company, you will receive return documentation summarizing the data collected and acknowledging that the appropriate form has been sent to the schools you listed. The forms to look out for are the Student Aid Report (SAR), based on the information you provided on the FAFSA, and the "Acknowledgement" and "Data Confirmation Report" from the College Board.

We want to make sure that this process goes as smoothly as possible for your family, so we have outlined what you should do and how you should do it. We've also provided examples of real African American families who have gone through this process, for better or for worse.

USE THE RIGHT FORMS

In order to qualify for financial aid, it is your responsibility to obtain all necessary forms and file them accurately and on time. First and foremost, you must find out which forms each school on your list requires. Some schools require their own supplemental financial aid forms in addition to the FAFSA and PROFILE, so obtain the appropriate forms where applicable. Both the FAFSA and the PROFILE include spaces where you will list the schools that require that particular form—so you only have to complete and file one copy of each.

The FAFSA: You must fill out the Free Application for Federal Student Aid if you wish to receive any federal aid at all. It can be filed only after January 1 and can be found in high school guidance offices, college financial aid offices, public libraries, www.fafsa.edu.gov, or by calling (800) 4-FED-AID.

The PROFILE: Private schools and some state schools require the CSS/Financial Aid PROFILE form. It is used to determine aid eligibility at schools that use the institutional methodology. To obtain a copy of the PROFILE, a student must register with the College Board and pay a processing fee. You can obtain registration information in high school guidance offices or register online at http://profileonline.collegeboard.com.

DEADLINE CONFUSION

Each form has its own deadline, and each school has its own set of deadlines for each form, so this can get pretty complicated. You'll want to keep track of these deadlines very closely.

Let's use Stanford's freshman deadlines as an example. Stanford requires the PROFILE, a Noncustodial Parent's Statement (if applicable), and a copy of your parents' tax returns. (Don't think you can get away with anything sneaky here!) Note the different deadlines for financial forms and the actual school application.

Stanford University's Deadlines for the 2003–2004 Application Season	
Early Decision	
Register for the CSS PROFILE	October 1, 2002
Application deadline	**November 1, 2002**
File the CSS PROFILE application	November 1, 2002
Submit noncustodial parent's statement to FAO	November 1, 2002
File FAFSA application	April 15, 2003
Submit parent 1040 tax return with W-2 forms to FAO	April 15, 2003
Regular Decision	
Application deadline	**December 15, 2002**
Register for the CSS PROFILE	January 15, 2003
File the CSS PROFILE application	February 1, 2003
Submit noncustodial parent's statement to FAO	February 1, 2003
File the FAFSA application	April 15, 2003
Submit parent 1040 tax return with W-2 forms to FAO	April 15, 2003

Source: Federal Register

You can see that the FAFSA application and tax returns are due at the same time, regardless of whether you apply early decision or regular decision; all other dates, however, are different.

The early-decision deadlines may cause some confusion at first: How can the PROFILE be due in November if parents may not even receive W-2s until the end of January, or later?

In cases like this, you must draft up an estimate of your tax returns and use the resulting figures on the PROFILE form. If your financial situation hasn't really changed in the past year, last year's tax returns would be a great place to start. You want to appear as needy as possible, so if you are uncertain about any figures, estimate the numbers in your favor. Just make sure your estimates are realistic. Remember to apply the strategies we discussed earlier to help lower your EFC if you think they are appropriate for your situation.

Your family will soon receive an estimated financial award letter. When you submit your FAFSA application and tax returns to the college a few months later, the necessary adjustments will be made, and the financial award letter will be finalized.

WHAT YOU'LL NEED TO FILL OUT THE FORMS

The numbers on your tax returns must correspond to the numbers on your need-analysis forms. Ideally, you should fill out your financial aid forms and tax returns at the same time; that way, you can apply EFC-lowering tactics before those numbers are set in stone on either form. Unfortunately, as in our Stanford example, this isn't always possible.

When you sit down to fill out the FAFSA, you need to give the form your devoted attention. Clear your calendar for the day. We recommend that parents and the student sit down to go through it together, so that you both have a good grasp of the joint project you've embarked on. You may want to fill out the FAFSA worksheet on www.princetonreview.com as a helpful warm-up. If you're filling out the form manually instead of online, have at least two copies of the FAFSA so that you can use one as a rough draft. Get all your documents together and make photocopies. Keep this book handy as you go through the form so that you can refer to the tips we've given.

The following lists detail the records you will need for filling out the need-analysis forms (excerpted from *Paying for College Without Going Broke*, by Kalman A. Chany with Geoff Martz).

If You've Already Completed Your 2002 Tax Return

1. Completed federal tax return (all schedules)

2. W-2 forms

3. Records of untaxed income (Social Security payments received, welfare payments, tax-exempt interest income, etc.)

4. Bank statements

5. Brokerage statements

6. Mortgage statements

7. Student's Social Security number and driver's license (if available)

8. If you are an owner of a business, the business's financial statement or corporate tax return

9. Any other investment statements and records

10. Record of child support paid to or received by former spouse

11. Records of medical and dental expenses (must have been actually paid or charged on your credit card during the base income year)

IF YOU HAVE NOT COMPLETED YOUR 2002 TAX RETURN

1. A blank copy of the 2001 federal income tax form

2. A copy of your federal return for last year (all schedules)

3. W-2 forms (If unavailable, you can probably get your employer to tell you the numbers, or you can figure them out for yourself from pay stubs. Remember to include any bonuses or overtime you received.)

4. Any 1099 forms (statements sent by an employer, brokerage house, bank, or the government to report income earned as an independent contractor, dividends, interest, unemployment benefits, or a refund on state and local taxes from the prior year)

5. If you are a self-employed, a record of all income received, and a record of all IRS-deductible business expenses

6. Records of untaxed income (Social Security payments received, welfare payments, tax-exempt interest, etc.)

7. Bank statements

8. Brokerage statements

9. Mortgage statements

10. Student's Social Security number and driver's license (if available)

11. If you are an owner of a business, the business's financial statements or corporate tax return

12. Any other investment statements and records

13. Record of child support paid to or received by former spouse

14. Records of medical and dental expenses (must have been actually paid or charged on your credit card during the base income year)

15. Record of any post-secondary tuition paid

AVOIDING MISTAKES

The African American FAOs we interviewed told us that the main pitfalls that plague applicants when filling out the need-analysis forms are:

- Incomplete and inaccurate information

- Late applications

These pitfalls cause delays, and in many cases they can lead to less aid—or none at all. You'll get a second chance to fix incomplete and inaccurate information, but there's no turning back the FAO's clock when your forms are late.

Note the Deadlines, and Meet Them

With all the different deadlines you will face from the different schools—from applying for aid to applying for admissions—it's easy to miss deadlines. Keep a chart that lists the deadlines for each college—this includes admissions deadlines and financial aid deadlines for all forms. Put it somewhere visible, like on your refrigerator. Whatever you do, make sure you meet the deadlines.

Except for those with rolling admissions policies, colleges usually process applications in batches. All the applications that meet the deadline go in together. If an application arrives even one day late, it will have to wait with all the other late arrivals until the first batch of applications is done.

What's really confusing is that the FAFSA instructions say you can file until June of the student's freshman year. Don't let this fool you. What this means is that if you filed the FAFSA in June, the federal processor would still crunch your numbers for that school year. But if you waited that long, the aid will be long gone because the school deadlines are much earlier.

Some financial aid consultants say it's best to file financial aid forms close to the deadlines so you don't give the FAOs extra time to nit-pick over your application. After all, FAOs can't really begin doling out the dough until after the deadlines, when they have all the on-time applications in front of them. According to this theory, if you file too early, the FAOs will have time to find issues that they might have otherwise overlooked and that could reduce your financial aid award. Similar logic applies to the notion behind filing your taxes close to the April 15 deadline to reduce the chances of an audit.

The African American FAOs we talked to say forget about all of that. They urge students and their families to file the forms (the FAFSA, PROFILE, the colleges' individual financial aid forms, the admissions form, whatever) as early as possible because they've seen too many deserving students lose out on financial aid because of missed deadlines.

We agree with the FAOs. Procrastination is a big no-no when thousands of dollars are at stake. We recommend that you file the FAFSA and other forms as early as possible after properly, neatly, and accurately completing them. If you apply the strategies we've discussed in this book, and you've been accurate and honest, you shouldn't have to worry about the FAOs nit-picking anyway. Don't take your chances by putting it off until the last minute.

LOOK OUT FOR THESE QUESTIONS

OK, so the form is in front of you, and you're reading it over. Most of the questions are self-explanatory, but a few may cause some confusion. According to the U.S. Department of Education, these are the six questions on the FAFSA in which applicants make the most mistakes:

- Adjusted gross income (AGI)

- U.S. income taxes paid

- Income from work

- Untaxed income

- Number of people in parent's household

- Number of college students in the household

The following is a breakdown of the mistakes that are typically made and how to prevent them:

Adjusted Gross Income (Lines 39 and 73)

To estimate, or not to estimate? Applicants who have not yet done their tax returns put their estimated AGI on the form. There's nothing wrong with this, unless these applicants fail to update the AGI on their Student Aid Report and with the colleges' financial aid offices once they actually finish their tax returns. It's crucial that you update your figures after you get your taxes done and receive your SAR. This updating process can be avoided altogether if your tax return is done before or during the completion of the need-analysis forms.

Another common mistake is including nickels and pennies as part of your AGI. Just round your AGI to the nearest whole dollar amount.

U.S. Income Taxes Paid (Lines 40 and 74)

This question refers to the amount of tax you were required to pay the IRS, *not* the amount of tax your employer took out of your paychecks. Don't use the amount from your W-2 form that says "Federal Tax Withheld." Use the amount of "taxes paid" from your tax return. If you don't have a current tax return, estimate this amount by using your previous year's tax return (if you think the numbers will be similar), then update the amount once your taxes are done.

Income from Work (Lines 76–77)

Applicants often leave this question blank, thinking it's the same as the Adjusted Gross Income (AGI). You should never leave a question blank, unless it specifically states that it is okay to do so. In this figure, you should include wages, business and farm income, 401(k) contributions, tax-deferred annuities . . . everything. If the number happens to be the same as your AGI, list the appropriate figure on each line. (If you did not receive any income whatsoever from wages or a business, enter a "0" on this line.)

Untaxed Income (Lines 78–79)

Many applicants do not realize that to fill in this line they need to also complete the worksheet on page 8 of the FAFSA. A lot of families just enter a "0" or leave it blank. Here, you must report any untaxed income that you or your children received, including earned income credit, if applicable, and any untaxed portion of your Social Security benefits.

Number of People in Parent's Household (Line 64)

The more family members you list here, the higher your income protection allowance will be. You should start with those who actually live in the house—parents, stepparents, and siblings. If Grandma and Grandpa live in the house and receive more than half of their financial support from the parents of the household, add them. If there are other siblings not living at home who receive more than half of their financial support from their parents, plug them into the equation too. And students, don't forget to include yourself.

Please note: You should not include an ex-wife or ex-husband, or a significant other of a parent or sibling—even if he or she hangs out at the house pretty frequently.

Number of College Students in the Household (Line 65)

Prior to the 2000–2001 school year, you could include in this number parents who were enrolled in college, graduate, or professional school at the same time as the student. That's over. This number now includes only the siblings who are dependent children and are in college at the same time, as well as the student who is actually applying for aid. So if you have a daughter who is a high school sophomore in public school, a daughter who is applying for college in the fall, a son who is a senior in college, and a husband in business school, the number of college students in your household is two.

OTHER EMBARRASSING MISTAKES

These mistakes may seem ridiculous, but FAOs tell us they happen all too often:

- Applicants sometimes fail to write their Social Security numbers legibly. The Social Security number is the student's key identification mark for the federal processor and the FAOs. A wrong or illegible number can cause serious delays in processing your student's financial aid.

- Applicants neglect to fill out the most up-to-date version of the form. Check for the current year at the top. If you fill out the previous year's form by mistake, the federal processor will think you are applying for the school year that is already in session.

- Applicants forget to sign the form.

REAL-LIFE STORIES FROM THE WORLD OF FINANCIAL AID APPLICATIONS

The African American FAOs and students we interviewed shared a few of their financial aid application war stories to help your family make well-informed choices. We believe these cases offer food for thought. The outcomes of these families' experiences are both positive and negative. To protect the privacy of everyone involved, we don't mention any real names or colleges.

THE PRICE OF PRESTIGE

Reverend Ford is a respected pastor in the community, and Mrs. Ford is a corporate executive who recently obtained a position that landed her a close-to six-figure salary. They wanted their only son to attend a prestigious private school. He was an excellent student who worked hard, and naturally, they wanted the best for him.

Reverend and Mrs. Ford had a high combined income but very little savings. The cost of the school was $39,000 per year, and the financial aid package from the school covered the family's need in full—but the Fords' need was calculated to be only $11,000! This left $28,000 per year for the family to cover out of pocket.

How was this couple going to cover their EFC? The FAO who dealt with their case told us that their plan was to take out a home equity loan. Their son would also take out unsubsidized student loans. Over the course of four years they were looking at covering at least $112,000 in costs, not including interest.

The FAO told us that it was actually Mrs. Ford's idea that their son should attend this particular prestigious private school. She said she understood the costs involved. The FAO said he implied to the parents that they might instead consider a less expensive yet highly respected public college in the same state. The FAO's rationale was that after obtaining a bachelor's degree elsewhere, their son could then attend graduate school at the prestigious private school, as he was planning to continue his education anyway. Mrs. Ford wouldn't hear of it. She vowed to take on the debt, and Reverend Ford agreed.

The Ford family made several very big mistakes. First, they didn't plan ahead and save for college. Second, Mrs. Ford increased the family income during the base income year, the year before their son would go to college. Then they made the mistake of considering only one college, so when the school failed to offer them a good financial aid package, they couldn't use other aid packages as leverage. They just didn't have a Plan B.

Unfortunately, if you can't reduce your EFC before you apply for financial aid, you'll likely be stuck with major loans. What else could the Fords have done to help pay their EFC? It's highly unlikely that they would have been able to gather even close to $100,000 in scholarships, and most of that money would have been used by the FAOs to readjust the aid package, without reducing their EFC. Still, if there was even the slightest chance of lowering their family contribution, the Fords should have searched for scholarships. What scholarships are available at Mrs. Ford's company or at Reverend Ford's church or its denomination's headquarters? Are the Fords members of any other civic groups such as fraternities, sororities, lodges, or unions?

Seek and Ye Shall Find

John James is a single father who paid for both of his daughters' college educations by researching every possible scholarship. A public high school teacher, making $53,000, he had graduated from college in the early 1970s when financial aid was plentiful and college was relatively inexpensive. The FAO of this public college told us that John had kept his eye on the rising costs of a college education and was determined that he would find free money for his daughters, who were two years apart.

John searched hard for scholarships. He used scholarship search services on the Internet, scoured reference books in the library, and bought books on scholarships and grants, including books specifically for African Americans. He applied for scholarships for African American students offered by organizations such as the United Negro College Fund and The Urban League, as well as community, church, and other organizations. He developed a relationship with the FAO, who willingly answered his questions and offered tips. Most of the scholarships he found could be applied toward reducing his EFC as opposed to covering need because they were disbursed directly to his daughters and not to the school's bursar's office.

"He applied to just about everything on behalf of his daughters whether he thought they had a shot of getting the scholarship or not," the FAO said. "He attended a financial aid workshop at their high school. Finding scholarships became like a hobby to him. The guy just really kept at it and ended up not paying for much of anything."

The Lord Will Make a Way

Sharon Bethel came from a poor family but had been accepted to an expensive, prestigious private college. She had fantastic grades. The oldest of six children, she was raised in a single-parent household by her mother, who had dropped out of high school and worked as a housekeeper at a hotel. Her mother's pride and faith in God was strong, and she pushed her daughter to be the best. She would be the first in her family to attend college.

Sharon was on her way to receiving a full scholarship. One problem: She never collected the money.

The FAO told us that Sharon filed her FAFSA but did not submit any of the other necessary documents—in this case, the PROFILE form and her mother's tax return. In addition, her FAFSA was incomplete and needed updated information. Once she received her acceptance letter from the admissions office, Sharon asked for an extension to send in the rest of the documents. But by the time she returned some of the documents, the extension deadline had passed. By that time, the school had already given away the scholarships and grants that were slated for Sharon. This needy student had missed out on a free ride. The FAO had to deliver the bad news.

"She still came to the school's summer program for incoming freshmen because she said her mother told her the Lord was going to make a way. But she never sent all of her stuff in. She would've gotten the money," the FAO said. "It's imperative that you apply on time."

Sharon's case illustrates how important it is to file forms accurately and on time. Sharon had the grades, and the college was going to give her the financial aid she needed to cover everything. God did in fact make a way. Sharon just failed to take the necessary steps through the doorway to claim her blessing.

THE PERFECT FAMILY

The Venerables had a combined income of about $52,000. Other relatives in their extended family had graduated from college, but neither Mrs. nor Mr. Venerable had attended. They had a seventeen-year-old son who was a junior in high school and a thirteen-year-old daughter in junior high. Their son would be the first in their immediate family to attend college.

Realizing that they didn't understand the financial aid process and that they didn't have much time, the Venerables attended a financial aid workshop at their son's high school. They brought their son along too.

An FAO was one of two experts invited to do the workshop. The FAO said that after the session was over, the parents struck up a conversation with him and asked intelligent questions about financial aid. The parents were very interested in what he had to say because their son wanted to attend the college the FAO worked for. They asked the FAO if they could follow up with him later.

"I really didn't expect to hear from them, but in January I got a call," the FAO said. "They were getting ready to fill out the FAFSA, and they asked more questions. That was really a beneficial approach to getting financial aid. They went and got the information and then attacked it in a timely manner. They asked me to review the form, and I did. They wound up getting everything that we could give them."

Clearly, this case shows what can happen when parents and students take the financial aid process seriously and educate themselves. Like you, the Venerables probably also bought books like this one and learned the necessary steps to pay for college. The key to their success is that once they got the information, they followed though.

A BUMPY RIDE

Tina Strong was an excellent high school student. She knew that she wanted to go to college to study medicine and figured she should have no problem getting a full scholarship. Tina's GPA was a 3.8 on a 4.0 scale. She took the SAT without the benefit of a prep course and scored a 1000. Tina decided she wanted to aim for a better score, so she took a prep course and then took the SAT again, this time scoring a 1200.

In her junior year in high school, Tina visited several colleges, including a few HBCUs. During one of her college visits, the admissions officer offered Tina a full academic scholarship right on the spot. Tina told us that the offer was made in December, before she had filled out the FAFSA, and when she also had her eye on a more prominent HBCU. She declined the offer, figuring she ought to explore more options first. After filling out the FAFSA, Tina and her parents were shocked to see the EFC amount on their SAR. Tina was ineligible for financial aid. Her mother had recently married, and according to the federal processor, her stepfather made too much money.

"I didn't know that money was going to be so important because that was before I applied for the scholarships," Tina said. "Before the FAFSA form went in, I didn't know I wasn't going to qualify for any financial aid. That was before they broke my heart and my pockets."

Tina told us she applied for a number of merit-based scholarships, but she received only $3,000—a mere drop in the bucket compared to the cost of the $24,000-a-year HBCU she wanted to attend. She narrowed her colleges down to two schools: the HBCU and an out-of-state private school. She eventually decided on the HBCU, but she made her decision after the college's deadline. Adding insult to injury, her delay meant the small financial aid package the college had offered her was now gone too.

Tina attended the HBCU anyway, but she and her parents had to take out about $18,000 in loans her freshman year because they had not saved for college. Feeling guilty about the financial burden Tina's college education was causing her family, she transferred after her freshman year from the college she loved to a less expensive in-state school. She hated the state school, and she and her parents still had to take out $11,000 in loans to cover the bill.

Now Tina is headed back to the $24,000 HBCU for her junior year, but she is upbeat about it. Regardless of the cost, she will be attending a great college that she adores. When it's all said and done, she and her parents will have more than $80,000 in loans to repay; they understand, though, that Tina's education is an invaluable investment that will increase her earning power for years to come. Because her eyes have been opened by the amount of money at stake, Tina says she is even more motivated to succeed.

"My college experience has been bumpy and challenging, but it's all working out," Tina said. "I'm trying not to make the same mistake when I go to grad school."

Tina's case shows how important it is to make informed decisions. Had Tina and her parents known that she would not be eligible for financial aid, they could've made better decisions earlier on. Had they known how their EFC would be determined, they might have been able to apply strategies to reduce it. Instead of rejecting the full scholarship offer from the first HBCU, Tina should have asked for a few months to consider the offer before notifying the school of her final decision. Once she received financial aid offers from the other schools, she could have used the full scholarship offer to negotiate a better deal with the FAO at her favorite school. Tina also could have attended the college that was willing to give her a full ride and gone to graduate school at her first-choice college, or she could've transferred to her first-choice school after a couple of years.

A Sloppy Student

We also heard about a very sloppy student who carelessly filled out his FAFSA and sent it in, thinking everything was cool. He received an acceptance letter from the school he wanted to attend. About a month after submitting the FAFSA, he received his SAR, which summarized the information he submitted and estimated his award amount.

We wish we could've talked to this student and told him to look over his SAR carefully for mistakes, informing the federal processor of any errors. Unfortunately, he never studied his SAR, and that's where all his trouble began.

Our sloppy student showed up on campus thinking he was good to go as far as financial aid was concerned. He had excellent grades, so he figured he had been given some decent grants and scholarships. His parents' low income and his lack of savings sealed the fact that his need was obviously high. There was just one small problem: the FAO had trouble finding the student in the system. Once he found his name, he noticed that the handwritten forms were difficult to read. Then he noticed the big problem: The student's Social Security number on his admissions form and other documents didn't match the number on his financial aid document, which was one digit off. Someone misread the sloppy student's messy handwriting on the FAFSA and entered the numbers incorrectly. "Oops, my bad. But where's my financial aid?" the student asked.

After a few nervous days and many trips back and forth to the financial aid office, the student did eventually get his aid. But he never had his Social Security number corrected. That wrong number followed him throughout his college career, and each year there were problems and delays with his aid.

Said Too Much

On the PROFILE form, a talkative student revealed that she "couldn't stand her daddy's new wife." This was inappropriate information to share with a financial aid officer, and besides—why would an FAO care about that? More importantly, her father's tax form didn't say anything about a new wife. Red flag!

When a family's EFC is calculated, the income of every adult living in the student's home counts—including a stepparent's. Whether the student liked the stepmother, the income of "daddy's new wife" could have had a major impact on this student's financial aid package. After some awkward questions and confessions, the student admitted that the "wife" was actually a woman her divorced father had been dating for a year.

The FAOs aren't the CIA or FBI. They don't want to know all of your personal business. Only reveal what is requested, and you'll avoid hassles like this one.

TIMELINE FOR COLLEGE AND FINANCIAL AID APPLICATIONS

Applying for college and for financial aid is tough, and there seems to be too much to keep track of. To help you out, we've broken down the process into more manageable pieces. Use this as a guideline, but remember to always use the schools' application materials as your primary source for scheduling and deadlines.

FINANCIAL AID TIMELINE: FRESHMEN AND SOPHOMORES

Too early to think about college? Think again! Even though it might seem as if you've just left the hallowed halls of junior high, there are things you can do now to pave the way for college success and earn more financial aid.

- Take challenging courses, and fill your schedule. More classes usually mean a better chance to hike up your GPA—assuming, of course, that you do well. Take courses that are prerequisites for upper-level courses, so you can really make the most of your junior and senior years.

- Three or four years of a foreign language looks great on a high school transcript—and it's also a good idea in general to expose yourself to another language. French, Spanish, and Latin are staples at many high schools, but your high school might offer others. Though you won't take the SAT for a year or two, it wouldn't hurt to start building your vocabulary. And studying hard for your English and math courses will make actual SAT prep that much easier later on.

- Get involved in extracurricular activities in your school or community. Colleges look at more than just the numbers on your transcript and SAT—they'll want to see how well-rounded you are too. So check out the band, athletic teams, or art club, and try to work your way up to a leadership role if possible.

FINANCIAL AID TIMELINE: JUNIORS

This is an important year for getting ready for college applications and financial aid. Here are some things you should be doing:

- Keep up those grades. Keep taking challenging courses, like AP and upper-level math and language courses. Colleges will really look at your junior and senior years to see how much you've been pushing yourself academically.

- Register and prepare for the SAT, SAT II, and/or ACT. Different colleges require different tests, so start looking into colleges that interest you. If you need another test, it's a good idea to get it out of the way now, although you'll have more opportunities to take them later on. (This way, you can retake them if you don't score as well as you'd hoped.)

- Think about earning and saving money, but keep in mind that unless your family is sure they'll be ineligible for aid, you shouldn't earn more than $2,436 (if your potential college uses the federal methodology) or $2,490 (if the college uses the institutional methodology). Most of your energy right now should be spent on keeping up your grades.

- Stay involved in those extracurricular activities—prolonged involvement in a few activities is more impressive than month-long stints in everything your high school offers.

- Now that you're an upperclassman, try to obtain some sort of leadership position—class president, trumpet section leader, team captain. Holding leadership roles shows your dedication and commitment.

- Send away for information from colleges you're interested in. Although you'll want to investigate further than the college brochures, they'll give you a good idea of the colleges' sizes, philosophies, locations, and demographics. And most will give you postcards, phone numbers, and contact information so if you decide to apply there, you can. You should also pick up a good college guidebook, like the Princeton Review's *The Best 345 Colleges*. Start getting familiar with the schools; make a list of those that jump out at you.

Summer Before Senior Year

- Now's the time to take another look at all those college brochures and college guidebooks. Look through Step 2 of this book and start figuring out which schools should make your shortlist. Try to get all the information you can about these colleges' application and financial aid requirements.

- Schedule college visits. You can visit in the fall, too, but you'll be surprised at how quickly application deadlines can approach. You might want to make more than one visit to schools you're especially interested in, and you'll want to have plenty of time to do so.

FINANCIAL AID AND COLLEGE APPLICATION TIMELINE: SENIORS

Ah, senior year. The Homecoming game and the Christmas dance may be fun, but senior year can also be stressful. This is when the big decisions about college must finally be made. Here's a brief summary of what you should be doing, and when.

Late Summer/Fall

- Make sure you visit colleges! You should have started doing this at the end of your junior year, so catch up if you're behind schedule.

September/October

- It might be tough to face it, but now is the time to start getting into the nitty-gritty of college selection. There are a lot of steps to go through before you can send in your application—writing essays, getting letters of recommendation, filling out the many forms—and a good way to relieve some of the stress is to stay ahead of the game.

- That said, start talking to your teachers or contacts in the community and see if they'll write your letters of recommendation. If they agree, and when you've decided where to apply, be sure to provide them with all the necessary documents: the form(s) from the college, the envelope from the college or a self-addressed stamped envelope, and a resume, if you have one. A list of activities and accomplishments will be fine too. You'll want your referees to know exactly what you've accomplished. And remember to give your writers plenty of time to complete your recommendations; thank them for the favor by respecting their busy lives and schedules.

- Check out college fairs and financial aid workshops offered by your high school or community. Your parents will probably want to come with you—let them! As we said in Step 1, college is a big step that affects the whole family. (And face it—your parents are most likely going to be the ones filing for financial aid!)

- Continue to visit schools that interest you.

- Take the standardized tests like the SAT or ACT if you haven't already; retake them if you want to try for a better score.

- Keep taking challenging courses, and keep your grades up. Admissions officers *do* notice if you start "coasting" your senior year!

November

- Chances are, your college applications are due soon. If you've stayed on top of things, you should be all ready to buckle down and get them done. Each one undoubtedly requires several components, so it's imperative that you stay organized. Make lists or charts of what you need to do for each application, and be sure to meet your deadlines!

- Be sure to check in with those who are writing your recommendation letters. They should be aware of your deadlines, too.

- Take the time to perfect your essays. Give them to your English teacher or another adult to critique, and be sure to have someone proofread them before you send them in. (We know one student who misspelled *background* in every one of her essays—*backround* sounded right, but a proofreader would say other-wise! Don't rely on your computer's spellchecker, either. It may not catch common errors, such as the difference between *your* and *you're*.

December

- Finish up any remaining applications, mail them off, and then breathe a sigh of relief. Once those applications are out the door, you can relax for a while.

January

- Now the financial aid process gets into full swing. You can obtain a FAFSA form after January 1. Sit down with your parents to discuss the cost of college and what this investment means to you and your family.

- Depending on your selected colleges' deadlines, your financial aid forms may be due this month. Note individual school deadlines for particular forms. If any schools require the PROFILE form, be sure to file it.

February

- Even though your high school transcripts went out to the schools already, some colleges will request your mid-year grades—again, senior year is *not* the time for coasting! The more selective schools, especially, will want to see that you're working hard even when you don't technically "have to."

- Keep watching deadlines for financial aid and scholarship forms.

March and April

- Early college acceptance letters may arrive in March; the rest will likely arrive in April. This is a stressful time of mailbox-watching, we know. But have confidence that you've put your all into your applications!

- In April, you'll receive financial aid offers along with letters of admission. Refer to Step 6 to figure out how to assess and respond to the offers.

- And finally . . . choose your college! Acceptance deadlines vary; make sure you don't miss yours.

Summer before Your First Year of College

- If you will be taking out student loans, work with your parents to obtain and file the necessary forms.

- Colleges may ask for your final grades; have your high school send them.

- Feel free to go out and get a job, but don't make too much money. Your wages will affect your EFC until the summer before your senior year in college. This is a great time to explore internships; they may not pay you much (or at all), but the experience they provide is a worthwhile trade-off.

STEP 6: ASSESS AND RESPOND TO THE FINANCIAL AID OFFER

By sometime in April, you should receive financial aid award letters from schools to which you were accepted. You may find that the offers contain figures that are pretty close to what you anticipated. You may be thrilled to receive a stellar offer or two. Or you may find yourself disappointed by one or more small, inadequate aid packages, teeming with loans. In addition, you may have unmet need.

"Where the heck am I going to find X thousand dollars?" you moan.

You don't have to accept the cards you've been dealt just yet, though. Push back at the FAOs and try to negotiate a better deal.

You weren't sure whether that was an option, right? It's one of the best-kept secrets around. You do not have to accept the first financial aid package the college offers you.

This is something we wish we had known when we were in college. Back then, we got our award letters year after year and felt grateful for whatever aid we received. We were happy to see federal work-study and guaranteed student loans listed on our award letters. We were relieved to be getting any aid at all, and we never gave much thought to how much money we would eventually have to pay back for the loans—including interest. But you know what? We probably could've gotten better aid packages if we'd only asked. We had strong cases for the FAOs: Both of us were great students. We were part of the first generation in our family to attend college, which means we should have benefited from the many grants and scholarships available to encourage first-generation students. Having grown up in one of New York City's poorest and toughest neighborhoods, Brownsville, Brooklyn, we were definitely needy.

They say (here *they* are again!) that hindsight is 20/20. Back then, we didn't know any better. But now *you* do!

THE AWARD LETTER

Working with the admissions office, FAOs consider how badly the college wants each student. They look at the family's ability to pay as well as the federal, state, college, and private aid available to meet the family's need. They then prepare and send a financial aid award letter.

The award letter spells out what types of aid the college is offering you, along with the dollar amount of each type per semester. Spend some time going over the award letter from each college. Review what you have learned about the different types of financial aid and ensure that you fully understand the terms of the college's offer.

The aid that is used to cover your need can include any combination of the following: grants, scholarships, federal work-study, state loans, college loans, Perkins loans, and *subsidized* Stafford loans. You should *not* see PLUS loans or unsubsidized student loans (including the Stafford) on the award letter. The loans are intended to help students and parents cover their expected family contribution. Figure 6.1 illustrates where each type of aid fits into the equation.

Figure 6.1 The Award Letter: What Goes Toward Your Need vs. Your EFC?

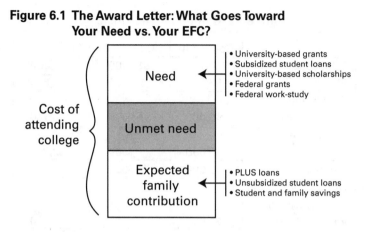

- University-based grants
- Subsidized student loans
- University-based scholarships
- Federal grants
- Federal work-study

- PLUS loans
- Unsubsidized student loans
- Student and family savings

COMPARING OFFERS

If you have received aid offers that just don't seem doable, don't rush to the phone to call the school and complain. Wait until you have received aid award letters from each and every one of the schools your student was accepted to. Inspect each award carefully, and note the amount that you will have to pay now (EFC) and later (loans). These figures are more important than the overall size of the package.

Compare schools that are equivelant in terms of academic quality. If the schools' packages are drastically different, something is probably amiss. Check out Figure 6.2, comparing the aid offers from three similar schools.

Figure 6.2 Comparing Aid Offers

	College A	College B	College C
Total cost	$20,000	$19,000	$15,000
EFC	$6,000	$6,000	$5,500
Grants and scholarships	$9,000	$12,000	$5,750
Need-based loans	$3,000	$500	$3,250
Work-study	$1,000	$500	$500
Unmet need (what parents will pay in addition to EFC)	$1,000	$0	$0
Value of the aid package	$13,000	$13,000	$9,500
Money the family will have to spend	$7,000	$6,000	$5,500
Need-based debt	$3,000	$500	$3,250

Source: Paying for College Without Going Broke, Kal Chany with Geoff Martz

Which do you think is the better deal? Is it College A because it costs the most, yet offered a $13,000 aid package? Is it College C because the family will have to pay the smallest expected family contribution? No and nope.

Assuming that the academic qualities of the schools are comparable, College B is the best deal. The total of the money the family will pay up front and the debt they will incur are less than the others. The cost of the school doesn't even really matter.

Should You Accept the Award?

Now that you have determined which schools are offering you the best packages, consider which schools are on the top of your student's list. Did your child's top-choice school make the weakest financial offer? If so, you may want to appeal the award.

Financial aid officers have to follow certain guidelines when they award aid, but they also have a good deal of flexibility within those guidelines to put together a generous package for the student. Often, the package they offer is *less* than what they can actually afford to offer. And they're really hoping that you'll accept it.

There are a few things to consider before you decide to appeal the package. Is your family able to comfortably pay the EFC and loans that have been laid out for you? If so, an appeal won't likely do any good. If you are feeling nervous that paying the college bill will seriously cripple you financially, you'll definitely want to give it a try. The worst thing that can happen is that the FAO can say no.

Study the different parts of the offer carefully. It's possible to accept some parts of the award letter and reject others. You should never reject any free money—grants and scholarships. You should also hold on to Perkins loans and subsidized Stafford loans because their interest rates are unbeatable; if the amount you are being loaned is incredibly high, though, you may be able to negotiate that part of the offer. If you see any PLUS loans or subsidized student loans appearing in your need coverage, perhaps you can request that these be replaced by grants or subsidized loans.

If you decide to accept the award, it doesn't mean that you have committed yourself to that college. It just guarantees that the money offered will be available, should you decide to attend.

APPEALING THE AWARD

The African American FAOs we spoke with shared a number of tips to help parents and students understand what influences FAOs to offer better aid packages. Their biggest tip? They prefer to talk to parents who are prepared and are educated about financial issues and who already have a plan in mind concerning what they will ask for. One FAO told us flat out, "If a person comes in and is educated about the financial aid process and they know what they want to do, that's impressive right there. It's more impressive than just coming in cold and saying, 'I need more money.' "

It's really important to have a clear idea of what you will request, including which specific parts of the offer you'd like the FAO to adjust and by how much. Do you want the FAO to reduce the amount of student loans and add more grants and scholarships? (Isn't that what we all want?) Do you want the FAO to allow at least a portion of an outside scholarship to go toward your EFC instead of your need? Has your financial situation changed so drastically that you need a reduced EFC amount? Make sure you know what you want—and have all of the supporting evidence and documentation in front of you before you get on the phone to call the FAO.

It's important to note that if you applied early decision to this school, appealing the award won't likely do much good. What incentive does the school have to make a better deal if they already know that you'll probably attend either way?

Legit Reasons for Requesting More Aid

The following are some legitimate circumstances that often persuade financial aid officers to give better aid packages. Be prepared to show proof of your claims with actual documentation, as the FAOs may request that you send or show them copies.

A Better Offer from a Comparable College

If you really want to attend School A, and similar School B made you a superior offer, you may be able to use School B's package as a bargaining chip. If your number-one school really wants you, the FAOs may match or exceed the competitor's offer.

The time to use this bargaining tool is *before* your student has committed to attend the school in the fall. If the student has already accepted, the college won't have much of an incentive to improve the package—they've got the student already. Even if you're certain you'll go to the school in the end, take your time. A hasty decision can cost you thousands of dollars in aid.

Loss of Employment

Some African American FAOs told us that many families are too proud to write or call the FAO to say that the husband or wife has recently lost a job. Don't be ashamed. Being truthful about what's happening with your finances can save you thousands of dollars.

Recent Illness or Death in the Family

FAOs often refer to illness and death as "special considerations" because they understand that under certain circumstances, paying the college bill is even more difficult. Most FAOs will be willing to make concessions and adjustments to your aid package if you encounter these misfortunes.

TIPS FOR A SUCCESSFUL APPEAL

Before the Call . . .

- **Check the size of the college's endowment.** This figure can usually be found on the college's website or by calling the school's business office. Find out whether the endowment is used to give money to deserving students. Your knowledge about the school's endowment will make you well prepared, which will impress the FAO.

During the Call . . .

- **Be courteous and direct.** Financial aid officers are very busy, overworked people handling many cases other than yours. Try to establish a relationship with the FAO you're speaking to. Be friendly and professional. Don't use potentially confrontational words like "negotiate," "bargain," or "deal." Instead, say you'd like to "appeal" the financial aid award. Make your appeal clear to the FAO, and be respectful. Being abusive, indecisive, or disorganized won't get you one extra penny.

- **Always highlight the student's skills.** Colleges want to invest in students who will become successful. Is your student gifted in music or other art forms? Is he a math whiz? Is she a top athlete or the first in the family to attend college? Schools theorize that when a student graduates and begins earning money, he or she will support the college and make alumni donations. If the student becomes famous, the college will benefit from having produced this "distinguished alumnus" who will inspire other students to attend the college. If you can show the FAO that your student has special gifts that may very well boost the school's reputation someday, the FAO will be impressed and will make more of an effort to give you the aid package you want.

- **Ask for an extension.** If you are near the deadline, ask for more time and make sure you write down the name of the person you spoke with. Follow up the phone conversation with a certified letter reminding the FAO of the conversation you had and what was agreed upon.

How to Kill the Deal

The following are two surefire ways to kill your chances of getting more money from the FAO:

1. Whine about credit card debt. If you tell the FAO you're strapped for funds because of high credit card bills or other consumer spending debts, they won't go for it. They'll figure that you *do* have the ability to pay, but that you just don't have your priorities straight. (Which is, as we said earlier, a fair assessment!)

2. Take an expensive flight to the school, drive up in a shiny new Lexus, or stroll into the office in the latest designer clothes. We're exaggerating to some extent, but you get the idea: now is not the time to appear wealthy. The FAO will figure you can afford the

financial aid package that was given to your student and suspect that you're just a greedy son of a gun.

GET THE FAOs ON YOUR SIDE

If you follow these tips, FAOs say they will go to bat for you, especially if you have "special considerations" that are causing your hardship. If your student has a strong academic record and special skills that indicate he or she can be a great benefit to the college, your chances of getting more free money and fewer loans are great. Have your appeal together and your documents in hand.

One of the FAOs we interviewed told us, "You really want to be straightforward with the financial aid officers you'll be working with for the next four years. If you make them mad and upset, they're really not going to fight for you if you need more aid. Just be straightforward, and we'll see what we can do."

COVERING YOUR EFC—SOLUTIONS FOR PARENTS

Regardless of whether these negotiations pan out, you'll still have an EFC to take care of. Here are some of the best and most common solutions for coming up with the money:

- **Pay up.** If you've been saving, this is the time to use the money. If you are hesitant about using some of your savings, remember that paying $5,000 now is much cheaper than paying $5,000 plus interest later on. If you can't manage to write a check for the entire amount of your EFC, contact your school about deferred payment plans or check out commercial organizations that offer this same service. The three largest of these organizations are:

Academic Management Services: (800) 635-0120
www.amsweb.com

Key Education Resources: (800) 539-5363
www.key.com/educate

Tuition Management Systems: (800) 722-4867
www.afford.com/Enrollment/schsearch.asp

- **If you own a home, use it.** A home equity loan is a line of credit that allows you to borrow against the value of your home. This may be a smart move for you, as the interest rates are low, you don't have to pay any interest until you write a check, and you get a tax deduction for interest paid. If you're applying to schools that use the institutional methodology, borrowing against your home also temporarily reduces your equity, which in turn lowers your assets and your EFC.

- **Take out education loans.** Federal programs are the largest providers. They often offer attractive rates when compared to other types of loans. Parents can take out PLUS loans without having to prove financial need, and you can borrow up to the total cost of your student's education minus financial aid received. Many lenders also offer private student loans. But because the federal government does not guarantee these loans, lenders assume a greater risk and charge higher interest rates.

- **Borrow from yourself.** Some 401(k) plans or pension plans allow parents to borrow up to half of the amount from their plan, with a cap at $50,000. Usually, these loans are repaid over the course of five years at a low interest rate. The upside: you're essentially borrowing from yourself, and in some cases, the interest you pay will go back into your account. The downside: you now have less money sitting in your plan and are, therefore, earning less interest.

Once you've figured out how to cover your EFC, you'll be an old pro. By this time next year, you'll be wishing you could do it all over again. And you will!

STEP 7: WHAT HAPPENS DURING COLLEGE?

If you make it through the freshman aid application process, we congratulate you. You're not through with financial aid yet, though. You'll have to reapply for every additional year you or your child is in college.

WHAT FORMS WILL I HAVE TO RESUBMIT?

You'll have to complete and file the FAFSA and PROFILE every year. Check with your college to see whether they require you complete any supplemental forms in addition to these two.

WILL MY AID PACKAGE REMAIN THE SAME?

Sometimes the aid package you receive as a freshman is renewable, and sometimes it isn't. Because the cost of college usually increases a few percent each year, your package will *at least* have to be adjusted to accommodate for rising tuition. If you want the financial aid office to remain generous and eager to service any financial emergency that may arise for you or your family, you need to maintain your grades and be on your best behavior. Some private scholarship awards disburse money to the recipient each year, but many are just one-shot deals that are disbursed in full only for your freshman year costs. Contact your FAO with any questions regarding your aid package, and stay in contact with them, because as the past year's economic downturn has shown us, your financial situation can change quickly and dramatically.

LOANS

If your freshman year financial aid package included Stafford of Perkins loans, your package may change over the course of the next few years. Unless you come upon a windfall (or serious financial distress) your EFC will probably change little from year to year. That means that the total amount of aid your college offers you every year isn't going to change much, either.

What *is* going to change is the sources from which that money comes. As an incoming freshman, a student is allowed to borrow only $2,625 in Stafford loans. Sophomores are entitled to $3,500, and juniors and seniors can borrow $5,500. Sounds like a real privilege, right? Not quite. The FAO may, and almost definitely *will*, adjust your package each year by replacing need-based grant money with loans, which means the amount of your total debt will increase. Don't be surprised when you see your need-based "scholarship" award go down your sophomore and junior years. It doesn't mean that you're not towing the line in the classroom; it just means that the financial aid office is doing its job. And that job is to make it possible for all of the school's students to continue their enrollment by using as little of the institution's money as possible. They'd prefer to loan you someone else's money (like a bank's). We're not saying that they *always* decrease your gift aid and replace it with self-help aid. But nine times out of ten, they do.

Independent students can borrow even more money than dependent students each year, but unfortunately, a specified portion of each loan amount must be unsubsidized.

WORK-STUDY

The amount of work-study in your financial aid package may also increase over the years. This is also considered self-help aid. It makes sense to assume that students are capable of putting in more hours of working once they're adjusted to college life, so prepare for this possibility. Your employer or FAO will consider your course schedule and grades when assigning your award, which determines the number of hours you can work.

ADDITIONAL OPPORTUNITIES

A few of the rules actually change in your favor as you settle into campus life.

SCHOLARSHIPS

You may find that as part of the campus community, you are now eligible for additional scholarship opportunities. Organizations such as Black Greek letter fraternities and sororities may offer monetary awards and scholarships for service, so investigate these options for any group or activity you participate in.

WAGES

Remember how we said that you could make only a certain amount of money the summer before your freshman year of college without being penalized? To review, you could make up to $2,436 without penalty if you were attending a public school; you could make $2,490 if you were attending a private school using the institutional methodology, although you'd still have to pay a minimum contribution of $1,150. Any extra wages would have been assessed at a ridiculous rate.

Truthfully, it takes a while for this situation to improve. As an upperclassman at a private school using the institutional methodology, you can make $2,815, but your minimum contribution goes up, too—to $1,400. All in all, you end up being allowed to make about seventy-five bucks more than you did in your freshman year.

Yet once you have filed that last financial aid form in the spring of your junior year, you are home free. Unless you plan to go on to graduate school right away (and have to apply for financial aid all over again), you can make as much as you'd like, without penalty, from the spring of your junior year until graduation.

SPECIAL CIRCUMSTANCES

If your financial situation changes drastically during the college years, you should inform the FAO at your child's school. If you lose your job or suffer some other financial loss, such as theft, report it to the FAO immediately; although he may not be able to alter the package that's already in effect, he will work with you to change the package for upcoming semesters.

Even if you lose money in an awkward and embarrassing situation, such as separation from your spouse, if it affects your financial situation, it's cause to alert your FAO.

BE A NAME, NOT A NUMBER

Students: once you get on campus, an important thing to remember is that you should have a good relationship with the FAO and the other staff in the financial aid office. They are busy people under pressure to process a lot of student information, and if you can avoid it, you don't want to become just a number on a manila folder. Many students complain that they've gotten the run-around in the financial aid office: one office worker tells you to fill out yet another form, while another sends you down the hall to the bursar or the admissions office. Now that you see the many steps it takes to process financial aid, maybe these inconveniences will seem a little more understandable! If the only time you go to the financial aid office is to complain about your aid, you can't expect a positive response, especially if your own negligence is the cause of the problem. No matter how inconvenienced you are—or how stressed your financial aid situation is making you—do your best to be friendly and direct.

Though financial aid is primarily about money, it's also about relationships. It would be to your advantage to have a good relationship with the financial aid folks at your school.

LOOK ON THE BRIGHT SIDE

Going through the financial aid process again can't possibly be as foreign and frustrating as it was the first time!

STEP 8: GIVE BACK

After four to five years of school, most college graduates will begin dealing with a number of major financial issues. Most will be transitioning into the world of full-time jobs, and many will feel the rush of finally having some money to burn. Others will go through the financial aid process again in the pursuit of post-graduate degrees. When students get caught up in the changes taking place in their lives, they sometimes lose sight of the importance of giving back—repaying loans and donating to your alma mater and organizations that support higher education.

YOU'RE NOT THE ONLY
ONE WITH LOANS

Loan repayment begins about six months after graduation, and it catches many graduates off guard. All of a sudden, a few hundred dollars a month are going toward a new bill. When you find yourself in this position, remember that you are far from being alone. According to the State PIRG's Higher Education Project study, *The Burden of Borrowing*, 64 percent of students graduated in 1999–2000 with student loan debt. The average debt among graduates was $16,928.

Specific Problems with Student Loan Debt for African Americans

We said in Step 1 that student loan debts are what we would consider "good debt." We didn't lie! But we do want to make you aware of the line where "good" student loan debt crosses the line into bad debt.

According to the State PIRGs' Higher Education Project, 84 percent of all African American students had student loan debt in 2000; the debt was typically $2,000 more than non-African American students. Twenty-two percent of African American college students come from low-income families, and 55 percent graduate with "unmanageable debt burden," meaning that they devote more than 8 percent of their monthly salary to loan repayment. The overall percentage of students graduating with unmanageable debt burden is only 39 percent.

These statistics are disheartening, but don't let them stop you from pursuing a college education. With these figures in mind, you can work smarter to get the best financial aid package you're entitled to and properly handle loan debt once you've graduated.

FINES, BAD CREDIT, AND WORSE

Monthly student loan payments can range from $50 to $300 or more. When you factor in rent or a mortgage, transportation, clothes, and food, the numbers can be intimidating. But you can't run from the responsibility. You owe it to the college you attended to pay it all back.

You also owe it to yourself; failure to pay back your loans can damage your credit rating. Just how will that affect your finances in the future? As you contemplate major purchases such as a car or a home, you will likely need some help financing these purchases. Finance companies turn to credit bureaus to determine how high of a risk you are. Credit bureaus take into account a number of factors—how much debt you have, whether you pay your bills on time, or at all—and assign you a high (good) or low (not so good) score, based on the rating system developed by Fair Isaac & Company, Inc. (FICO). If you apply to take out a loan, it is this score that determines the interest rate and other terms of the loan; if your FICO score is low on the finance company's rating scale, the company can reject you or jack up your interest rate.

If you fail to repay your student loans, you can bet your FICO score will go down and your credit will be hurting. We're going to give you the information you need so this won't happen.

REPAYMENT OPTIONS FOR FEDERAL LOANS

There are five ways to repay a federal subsidized loan or PLUS loan:

1. **The Standard Repayment Plan** requires fixed monthly payments (at least fifty dollars) over a set period of up to ten years. The length of the repayment period depends on the loan amount.

2. **The Extended Repayment Plan** allows loan repayment to be extended over a period of twelve to thirty years, depending on the total amount of the loan.

Borrowers pay a fixed amount each month (at least fifty dollars), but monthly payments will usually be less than those paid under the Standard Repayment Plan. Repayment may be more manageable, but borrowers will pay more interest over the duration of the repayment period.

3. **The Graduated Repayment Plan** allows payments to start out low and increase every two years. This can help borrowers whose incomes are low initially but will increase steadily. The repayment period will be anywhere from twelve to thirty years, depending on the total amount of the loan.

4. **The Income Sensitive Plan** is available only to borrowers who took out Stafford or PLUS loans from private lenders. The plan starts out with small loan payments that are adjusted annually, according to income. The lender and borrowers work together to establish a payment system.

5. **The Income Contingent Repayment Plan** adjusts monthly payments based on the borrower's income and the total amount of direct loans. As income rises or falls, monthly payments will be adjusted accordingly. Borrowers have up to twenty-five years to repay; after twenty-five years, the unpaid amount is discharged, but borrowers must pay taxes on the discharged amount.

Factors to Consider When Choosing a Repayment Plan

First, make a monthly budget to determine what you can afford. A budget will show your income and expenses and what's left over. Don't choose a plan just because it has the lowest monthly payments because the lower the payments, the more interest you'll pay. You can switch plans at any time.

Consider these strategies:

Loan Consolidation

You have the option of consolidating your loans or combining your eligible federal loans into one new loan and making only one monthly payment. In July 2002, student loan rates dropped to 4.06 percent for guaranteed student loans and 4.86 percent for PLUS loans; this is the lowest the rates have ever been, making it a great time to consolidate.

Postponing Repayment

Repayment can be postponed through deferment or forbearance. Deferment allows postponement of payments for a limited amount of time under certain conditions, such as financial hardship; students may request deferment if they find themselves unable to make the monthly payments due to such hardship. Forbearance allows the borrower to suspend payment or make smaller payments than originally scheduled for a limited period of time.

Prepaying the Loan

As a student loan borrower, you always have the option of paying more than your monthly payment without penalty. Prepayments are applied first to any charges or collection costs, then to outstanding interest, and finally, to principal. If the account is current, the prepayment will go toward the principal. This means you'll accrue less interest, and you'll be out of debt ahead of schedule. You don't have to sign up for this option or request permission—you can simply pay more than the required amount at any time during repayment.

LAST RESORTS

Loans are a fact of life for most students, and with careful planning and commitment, most students pay them off successfully. However, there are certain circumstances that can arise that make repayment impossible. In those cases, your loans will be **discharged**.

A discharge releases the borrower of all obligations to repay the loans. Proof of the following is needed:

- You become totally and permanently disabled

- You are unable to complete a course of study because your school closes or your eligibility was falsely certified by the school

- Your obligation to repay a loan is discharged in bankruptcy (this rarely happens)

- You die

DEFAULTING ON LOANS

If you fail to make timely payments, you will be considered delinquent. If you miss payments for 270 days, the loans go into

default. Defaulting on your loans is serious business, and it can lead to the following:

- The Department of Education will immediately demand repayment of the total amount due

- The Department of Education will attempt to collect the debt and may charge you for the costs of collecting

- The default will be reported to national credit bureaus, which will damage your credit rating and make it difficult to obtain financing for homes, cars, and other major purchases

- You'll become ineligible for deferments

- The Internal Revenue Service will withhold your federal income tax refund

- Wages may be garnished

School Default Rates

Students who fail to repay loans hurt not only themselves, but also the schools that they attended. A school's default rate is based on what percent of the loans taken out by its students are actually repaid; a high default rate can have a negative impact on federal and state aid. This is a particularly serious issue for public colleges, as they depend more on federal and state funding than do private colleges. If a school's default rate is high, the amount of financial aid loan money set aside for the college will drop. The college, in turn, will have less financial aid funds to give to needy students in the future.

In 1999 and 2000, there was a rumor spreading over the Internet that fourteen HBCUs (most of them in Texas) were going to be closed forever. The rumor blamed Texas's then-Governor George W. Bush for the "conspiracy" to kill all HBCUs, causing an uproar in the African American community.

None of this was true. What really happened was that Sallie Mae, the federal government's student loan corporation, had released a report stating that the HBCUs were at risk of losing federal financial aid for their students by 2002. The schools' default rates had risen above 25 percent.

The cause of all this drama was deadbeat students. To help the schools avoid losing their aid, Sallie Mae offered a plan of action, which, among other things, suggested requiring freshmen to take a debt management course. By 2001 the Department of Education announced that default rates were declining and that the at-risk HBCUs had been removed from the "watch list."

Don't be a deadbeat student. Take control early on in the process, and establish a budget. Contact your lenders to figure out the best repayment plan for you. Being responsible about paying your loans is part of the larger goal we encourage you to strive for—building wealth. You'll be helping yourself *and* future students who will be seeking the benefits of a college education.

A NOTE ON "CAREER STUDENTS"

A former college FAO who now counsels students told us that one of her pet peeves is "career students." These are students who linger in college seemingly forever, taking out unsubsidized non-need-based student loans year after year, and strategically dropping classes during the semester so they can keep qualifying for more student loans. Instead of using the loan money to invest in their education, they spend it on items such as cars, clothes, jewelry, or vacations. They take much longer than necessary to graduate—if they graduate at all. Then, sure enough, six months after they've (finally) left school, the first student loan bill arrives. Don't be a career student—the debt will catch up with you eventually.

SUPPORT SCHOOLS AND FUTURE STUDENTS

As we've gone through the process of writing this book and helping our sons prepare for college, alumni donations have been mentioned in nearly every conversation we've had. Over the years, we've heard many of our peers passionately express why they don't give to their alma mater. HBCU graduates often cite bad experiences they had with school administrators, or say that their college's alumni association fails to reach out to them. Colleagues from predominantly white colleges often say they don't feel a strong emotional attachment to the schools and that their money isn't missed.

Firm statistics on alumni giving are hard to find; after all, no school with a poor alumni donation rate would want to publicize that information. Dr. Marybeth Gasman, assistant professor of Higher Education at Georgia State University, has researched giving within the African American community and has written numerous articles about HBCUs. In a forthcoming book titled *Supporting Alma Mater: Successful Strategies for Securing Funds from Black College Alumni,* Gasman and co-author Sibby Anderson-Thompkins explore the key points concerning this issue.

Comparing HBCUs and predominantly white colleges, Gasman estimated that a few HBCUs receive strong support from nearly 50 percent of their alumni, but overall only about 10 percent of HBCU alumni give back at all; meanwhile, an average of 20 percent of alumni at predominantly white institutions (including whites, blacks, and other non-whites) give back.

Despite this estimate, which has earned the support of some presidents and leaders in the black college community with whom we spoke, there is a strong tradition of giving in the African American community. According to the National Center for Charitable Statistics, African Americans donated a higher percentage of their income to charity than whites or Hispanics in 2000–2001.

Minority Giving in the United States, 2000–2001 (Homeowners), National Center for Charitable Statistics					
	National overview	West	Midwest	South	Northeast
Average regional share of income donated to charity	3.50%	3.50%	3.10%	4.20%	2.70%
Predominantly white neighborhoods	3.30%	3.40%	3.00%	4.10%	2.50%
Predominantly black neighborhoods	5.10%	4.20%	4.80%	5.20%	5.00%
Predominantly Hispanic neighborhoods	3.80%	3.40%	2.80%	4.30%	4.30%

Gasman's research suggests that African Americans and white Americans tend to have different motives for giving. For example, in a black church, a person will likely give if he or she likes and supports the pastor or if asked by a clergy member; in a white church, less solicitation occurs, so donation requests don't make as much of a difference. In the community, blacks tend to give in response to crisis situations, while white donations tend to be motivated by prestige.

This pattern carries over to higher education as well. Gasman said that the average HBCU alumnus or alumna donates to the college if he or she highly regards the president, while alumni at predominantly white colleges give based on the reputation of the school. What the alumni think of the president is not as important as, for example, how well the school's sports teams are playing.

HBCU alumni also tend to seek a more personal touch from their school, such as a couple of phone calls or a thank-you letter. HBCUs "often have a small infrastructure for giving and development, and writing thank-you notes takes a lot of time and staff, so that's a big problem," Gasman explained. "Predominantly white schools on average are usually much better staffed in this area, but they tend to ignore their own black alumni altogether."

This lack of response from schools leaves black alumni feeling upset. "Black alumni are a little more skeptical of institutions," said Gasman, based on interviews she conducted for her book. "They say things like, 'I gave money and they never told me what happened to the money. I never got a thank you and I won't give again because of it.'"

Gasman thinks that while there are obvious ways white colleges can appeal to their black alumni, many of them don't explore these options. For example, during alumni telethons, they should ask black students to call black alumni so they can connect in the same way a female student might connect with female alumni.

They could also target the Black Greek letter fraternities and sororities because unlike their white counterparts, these organizations provide lifelong affiliations that stretch far beyond graduation. "When you send out an alumni publication [to black alumni] and all the people on the cover are white, what kind of message does this send?" Gasman added. "I think some people just operate so much in a white world that it doesn't register with them."

Well, it doesn't matter if you attended an HBCU or a predominantly white college: African American alumni need to give back to their colleges. Alumni donations help schools fund programs, provide student grants and scholarships, and make capital improvements to keep the campuses modern and up to date. This support enables colleges to recruit top African American students who will eventually join the alumni ranks, representing their schools. The funding also goes toward giving marginal high school students the opportunity to attend college—to develop and mature on campus and reach their potential. Alumni donations also provide college presidents with ammunition to successfully raise funds from corporations and other major funding sources. When these funding sources consider offering a school some financial support, they evaluate the strength of the school's alumni support. If alumni aren't donating, other sources will likely deny funding. They'll figure that if the students who attended the school don't support it, why should they?

There are other advantages to giving too. It provides alumni with a powerful voice and the opportunity to affect positive change. College trustees listen to alumni who have strong records of giving. There are also tax advantages to donating, so why not give to the noble cause of helping schools develop future leaders?

MANY WAYS TO GIVE

There are a number of ways for African American college graduates to give back. Join alumni associations and give annually. Support special fundraising projects. Set up a scholarship or endowment, or if you can afford to give only a little, any amount can make a difference.

Colleges make the process of donating really easy. Some colleges even allow you to donate online at their websites, deducting donations from credit cards or bank accounts. Through a partnership with NAFEO (National Association for Equal Opportunity), an organization that advocates for HBCUs, and banking giant Wells Fargo, alumni and friends of HBCUs can donate directly to the individual colleges through www.blackvoices.com.

The Tom Joyner Foundation (www.tomjoyner.com/foundation) is a key organization that raises funds for needy students at HBCUs. Established by popular radio personality Tom Joyner ("The Fly Jock"), the foundation selects a school each month to be the benefactor of the donations. Every dollar of the money raised is given directly to the school and its students, and the funds are administered through the financial aid office.

The Thurgood Marshall Scholarship Fund, named for the civil rights giant and first African American Supreme Court justice, provides scholarships for students attending public HBCUs (www.thurgoodmarshallfund.org).

The oldest and most well-known organization devoted to African American college students, the United Negro College Fund (UNCF; www.uncf.org), provides scholarships for students at selected private HBCUs and predominantly white colleges.

The National Urban League (www.nul.org) also provides scholarships each year as part of its Campaign for African American Achievement.

FINAL WORDS

As we help our sons prepare for college, we see our futures as well as our pasts. We envision them rising from our shoulders as we pass on the knowledge and wisdom shaped by our college experiences. We want them to follow their own roads to success but not have to stumble over the bumps we did along the way. When you give back, you're actually lending to the future—to someone else's journey—while repaying a debt that someone once invested in yours. Remember your responsibility.

CONCLUSION

They say the college years are the best of your life. And in this case, usually *they* are right. Everyone deserves a college education—no matter how rich or poor the person is. We hope one thing you take away from this book is the confidence to go after the schools you love, with the knowledge that money is out there to help you pay the bill. If you've taken this information to heart, you're ready to go after the financial aid you deserve. Good luck.

APPENDICES

APPENDICES

FAQS

1. **What is the difference between a grant, scholarship, and loan?**

   A grant is money given to you (usually by the federal or state government or the university) to pay for college costs. Grants are typically awarded on the basis of need. Scholarships are usually awarded by organizations or universities on the basis of merit (good grades, athletic skill, or some other talent or accomplishment). Loans are funds awarded by the government but are owned by third-party lenders. (Sallie Mae is the largest higher education lending institution.) The most important difference is that grants and scholarships do not have to be repaid, but loans do.

2. **What is the best type of financial aid?**

   The best type of aid is money that is free (no interest payments involved) and that you don't have to pay back. In other words, scholarships and grants are the best.

3. **What is the difference between your income and your assets?**

   Assets are investments that have the potential to produce money. This is very different from income, which is money received for labor.

4. **What is a balance sheet?**

   A balance sheet is a document that looks at the difference between income, expenses, assets, and liabilities and reveals cash flow and net worth. The three most important lines on a balance sheet are the top line, the bottom line, and net worth. The top line shows your salary and income from assets, the total amount of what you make. The bottom line shows what's left after you've paid taxes, expenses, and so on. Net worth tells you the difference between the values of your assets and the liabilities you owe. The most important of these lines on the balance sheet is the net worth line, not the income line. It is the barometer of your wealth.

5. What is the difference between assets and liabilities?
Assets are things you *own*. Liabilities are things you *owe*.

6. Which is better, a historically black college or university (HBCU) or a predominantly white school?
It depends on the student. African American students have excelled at both types of institutions. There are about 100 HBCUs, and there is a great deal of variety among them. Dig behind the perceptions, stereotypes, and images projected by people who claim to know what they are talking about, and discover for yourself which environment is best for YOU.

7. Are two-year colleges a good possible alternative?
Yes. Junior colleges usually have nonselective admissions and are often very affordable. The classes are much smaller than many colleges and universities. Like four-year colleges, two-year colleges are not all equal. There are definitely some lemons out there. You need to check the schools out carefully.

8. Do I really have to visit schools?
We highly recommend you do. Visiting the school will give you a good feel for what it will be like to live and study there for the next four to five years of your life.

9. **How many schools should I pick?**

Select about seven colleges from among three groups of schools. Group one is colleges that may appear to be a bit out of reach but would be a good places for you if you were accepted—your dream schools. Group two is schools that you have a good shot of getting into. Among this group might be in-state public universities or less expensive out-of-state schools. Group three should be your fallback or "safety schools." These are schools to which, based on your test scores (SAT or ACT) and your high school GPA, you are just about guaranteed acceptance. Make sure you spend time selecting your safety schools carefully because you just might find yourself going to one of them.

10. **What are some basic forms of college funding?**

- Federal and state government grants and loans

- Private sources such as fraternities, sororities, civic groups, unions, corporations, churches, and other organizations (for example, the The Tom Joyner Foundation, Thurgood Marshall Scholarship Fund, the United Negro College Fund, etc.)

- Institution-specific need-based and merit aid

- Personal (family) resources

11. **What's the difference between a subsidized and unsubsidized loan?**

A subsidized loan does not accrue any interest while you are in college (actually it does, but the government pays it for you), whereas an unsubsidized loan *does* accrue interest.

12. **What is an FAO?**

    FAO stands for *financial aid officer*. This is the person from the college whose job it is to determine what your financial aid package will be.

13. **What is the EFC?**

    EFC stands for *expected family contribution*. This is the amount colleges expect the parent and student to be able to pay out-of-pocket for college expenses.

14. **How is the EFC determined?**

    Based on the information you provide on the FAFSA, the federal processor determines your EFC by using a fairly complicated formula that takes into account a number of factors. The formula does not consider the price tag of the college, so whether the school's tuition is $5,000 or $20,000, your EFC will be about the same.

15. **What is the "base income year"?**

    This is the tax year prior to the one in which the student enters his or her freshman year of college. This year sets the financial aid tone for the remaining four to five years of college, so you want to look as needy as you can in this year.

16. **Should I think about cost when I'm trying to pick the right college for me?**

    No. Throughout the college search process, it's better if students do not concern themselves with the cost of the schools. The student should not be discouraged or intimidated by the numbers. It's important that students strive to attend the best college possible regardless of the costs.

17. **Can I ask for a better financial aid package?**

    Yes. You can ask for a better deal. You don't have to accept the first aid package the college offers you.

18. **Do I have to accept the entire financial aid package, or can I reject parts I don't like?**

Another little-known fact is that you can accept only parts of the award letter, which of course means that you can reject others. So you could accept the Pell and Supplemental Educational Opportunity Grants and reject the loans the school offers you.

19. **Do FAOs have the authority to make changes to my financial aid package?**

They sure do. The have great flexibility to award certain federal grants and school loans at their discretion.

20. **What are some reasons I can use to successfully appeal my financial aid award?**

FAOs may be willing to make a deal if the student has a better offer from a comparable school and the first college really wants the student. Special considerations, such as loss of employment or high debt payments due to a recent illness or death in the family, are also strong reasons for FAOs to improve your package.

21. **When do you begin repaying student loans?**

Usually about six months after you graduate, leave school, or are registered below full-time status at school. If you continue on to graduate school you may be able to get a deferment, meaning you won't have to begin making payments until after you've finished.

22. **Do I have to pay my loan back all at once?**

No. You can choose from a number of repayment plans allowing you to pay a certain amount per month over a period of years.

23. What if I can't repay my loan?

If you absolutely cannot afford to make loan repayments, you may obtain a forbearance or deferment depending on what your situation is. You will have to prove that you can't make payments, and this may include you having to disclose your finances. That can be very unpleasant. If you go on to graduate school, you can have your payments deferred. If you are experiencing financial hardship, you can get a forbearance.

24. What is a default rate?

This is the rate at which students from your college fail to repay their student loans. If a school has a high default rate, the federal government might not fund any more new student loans for current students at that school.

25. Why is it so important that I donate to my alma mater?

Alumni donations help colleges to fund academic programs, provide students with grants and scholarships, and make capital improvements that keep the campuses modern and relevant in changing times.

GLOSSARY OF TERMS

A.A. or A.A.S.: Acronyms for "associate of arts" and "associate of applied science" degrees, which can be obtained at a two-year community college, also known as junior college.

Achievement Test: Tests offered in areas of study such as English, science, and math, that many colleges use to help determine admissions.

ACT: The American College Testing exam. Many colleges in the South and Midwest require students to take this achievement test to determine admissions.

AGI: Adjusted gross income.

B.A. or B.S.: Acronyms for "bachelor of arts" and "bachelor of science" degrees, which can be obtained at four-year colleges and universities. The type of degree granted depends on the type of courses taken.

base income year: The calendar year before the academic year that financial aid is being sought for.

Business/Farm Supplement: An aid application required by a few colleges for students whose parents own businesses or farms or who are self-employed.

campus-based programs: Refers to Perkins loan, Supplemental Educational Opportunity Grant, and federal work-study programs, the three federal student-aid programs that are administered directly by the school's financial aid office.

College Board: The nonprofit organization that writes and processes the CSS Financial Aid PROFILE form.

community college: A junior college that does not have residential facilities for students and that is often funded by the government.

cooperative education: A program that combines periods of academic study and paid employment relevant to the student's field of study.

cost of attendance: An estimate by the school that includes tuition, fees, room, board, books, transportation, supplies, and personal expenses.

default: Failure to repay a loan according to the terms of the promissory note.

default rate: The percentage of students from the same school who took out federal student loans but failed repay them.

dependent student: A student who is considered to be dependent upon his or her parents for financial support.

dividends: Payments of part of a company's earnings to shareholders (people who hold stock in the company).

Educational Testing Service (ETS): The organization that writes the SAT exam.

employment allowance: A deduction against income in the federal and institutional methods for working parents.

expected family contribution (EFC): The amount of money the family is expected to contribute to the student's education costs. The EFC is used with the cost of attendance to determine the amount of financial aid the student needs.

FAFSA: Free Application for Federal Student Aid. This is the need-analysis form students must fill out to determine eligibility for financial aid.

FAO: Financial aid officer. This is the individual at the college who determines student financial aid packages.

federal methodology: Generally accepted method used to calculate the family's EFC. Most public schools apply this method to determine distribution of federal funds.

federal work-study: Program that gives students money for part-time work during the school year as part of their financial aid package.

financial aid: Money from a variety of federal, state, and private sources to help students pay for college. The basic forms are grants, scholarships, loans, and work-study jobs.

401(k), 403(b): Types of deferred compensation plans where employees defer part of their salary until a later date. The employer usually matches a percentage of the amount the employee defers. Meanwhile, the money is invested, and the employee doesn't have to pay taxes on this money until it's withdrawn. Parents may borrow from these plans to help cover college costs.

gift aid: Grant or scholarship to the student that the student does not have to repay.

grants: Gift aid that is usually given based on the student's level of need.

HBCU: Historically black colleges and universities. These institutions were established before 1964 with the intention of serving the African American community

independent student: This student is self-supporting and is not considered dependent on his or her parent(s) for financial support.

income protection allowance: A deduction against the parents' and student's income.

institutional forms: Supplemental forms used with the FAFSA by colleges to determine the student's eligibility for financial aid.

institutional methodology: Method generally used by private colleges to calculate the family's EFC.

interest: The amount money earns when it is invested. It is also the charge for a loan, usually a percentage of the amount of money loaned.

investment: The act of using money for something that will, over time, earn interest. Also, it's a commitment to something over a period of time.

junior college: An institution offering a two-year course program that is usually equal to the first two years of a four-year undergraduate course program and that leads to an associate's degree.

NAFEO: National Association for Equal Opportunity. The organization is an association of HBCUs. NAFEO's implements programs and policies to boost minority student enrollment and to strengthen HBCUs. (www.nafeo.org)

need: The amount of financial aid a student can get based on the student's EFC and the cost of the college. Need is determined by subtracting the EFC from the cost of the school.

open admissions: When a college admits most or all of the students who apply.

parent's contribution: The amount of money the parent(s) is expected to give towards the student's college bill.

PLUS loan: Parent Loans for Undergraduate Students. Federally subsidized program that allows parents to borrow money to help cover their EFC.

Pell Grant: Federal need-based money that is given to undergraduates who are usually lower or lower middle income. The program used to be called BEOG.

postsecondary: Education that occurs after high school, such as two- or four-year colleges and vocational and technical schools.

principal: The face value of the amount of money you put in savings or investments, or the amount of the loan you borrowed, not including interest.

PROFILE form: A need-analysis document that is processed by the College Board in Princeton, N.J.

promissory note: The legal document the borrower must sign to get a loan; it spells out the exact terms of the loan.

PSAT/NMSQT: PSAT is an acronym is for the Preliminary Scholastic Aptitude Test, a practice test usually given to high school students in the tenth and eleventh grades in preparation for the SAT (Scholastic Aptitude Test). The test also serves as the National Merit Scholar Qualifying Test.

ROTC: Reserve Officer Training Corps program. This is a training program to prepare college students to be commissioned officers in a branch of the U.S. military.

SAT: The SAT is a standardized college admissions test that measures the student's ability in math and reading.

SAR: Student Aid Report. The SAR is provided to students who fill out the FAFSA.

scholarship: A form of financial aid gift money that is usually given based on merit.

SEOG: Supplemental Educational Opportunity Grant. SEOG is a federal award given to students who have tremendous need.

simplified needs test: A method used to determine the family's EFC, where all the family's assets are excluded from the formula, usually if the family's adjusted gross income is less than $50,000.

Stafford loans: These are need-based and non-need-based student loans offered by the federal government. The subsidized Stafford loan is based on need and the government pays the interest while the student is in school. The unsubsidized Stafford loan is not based on need. The amount is used to cover the EFC. Interest accumulates on the loan while the student is in school.

student contribution: The amount of money the student is expected to pay toward his or her college bill.

Thurgood Marshall Scholarship Fund: Named for Justice Thurgood Marshall, the fund aims to support exceptional merit scholars attending public HBCUs. The fund was established in 1987. (www.thurgoodmarshallfund.org)

Tom Joyner Foundation: Founded by radio personality "The Fly Jock" Tom Joyner, the foundation provides money directly to the historically black colleges and universities (HBCUs) for the purpose of helping these students complete their education. Each month the Tom Joyner Foundation selects a specific HBCU as the benefactor of funds raised during that month. The money is sent directly to the school and the students. Scholarships are awarded through the financial aid department at the HBCU based on financial need and academic achievement. (www.tomjoyner.com/foundation/)

transcript: A list of all the courses the student has taken and grades received.

tuition: The amount of money colleges charge for classroom instruction and use of school facilities.

UNCF: United Negro College Fund, also known as "The College Fund." Established in 1944, the organization aims to enhance the quality of education for black students at HBCUs and other colleges by providing financial assistance, as well as raising operating funds for its thirty-nine-member private HBCUs. (www.uncf.org)

verification: The process by which the financial aid office requires additional documents to make sure information is reported correctly on financial aid forms.

INDEX OF HBCUS

Gadsden State Community College—Valley Street Campus
256-549-8200
www.gadsdenst.cc.al.us
webmaster@gadsdenstate.edu

Miles College
205-929-1661
www.miles.edu
adm@mail.miles.edu

Oakwood College
800-824-5312
www.oakwood.edu
admission@oakwood.edu

Shelton State Community College—Fredd Campus
205-391-2211
www.sheltonstate.edu/sscc

Stillman College
800-841-5722
www.stillman.edu
admissions@stillman.edu

Talladega College
256-761-6219
www.talladega.edu
be2long@talladega.edu

Trenholm State Technical College
334-420-4200
www.trenholmtech.cc.al.us
mcarter@trenholmtech.cc.al.us

Tuskegee University
334-727-8500
www.tusk.edu
admis@acd.tusk.edu

ARKANSAS

Arkansas Baptist College
501-374-7856
arkbapcol.edu
ahightower@swbell.net

Philander Smith College
501-370-5221
www.philander.edu
admission@philander.edu

University of Arkansas/Pine Bluff
870-575-8486
www.uapb.edu
fulton_e@uapb.edu

DELAWARE

Delaware State College
302-857-6353
www.dsc.edu
admissions@dsc.edu

DISTRICT OF COLUMBIA

University of the District of Columbia
202-274-5010
www.udc.edu
mnewman@udc.edu

FLORIDA

Bethune–Cookman College
386-481-2600
www.bethune.cookman.edu
admissions@cookman.edu

Edward Waters College
904-366-2529
www.ewc.edu

Florida A and M University
850-599-3796
www.famu.edu
bcox2@famu.edu

Florida Memorial College
800-822-1362
www.fmc.edu

Albany State College
229-430-4646
www.asurams.edu
fsuttles@asurams.edu

Clark Atlanta University
404-880-8000
www.cau.edu
admissions@panthernet.cau.edu

Fort Valley State College
912-825-6307
www.fvsu.edu

Morehouse College
404-215-2632
www.morehouse.edu
admissions@morehouse.edu

Morris Brown College
404-739-1560
www.morrisbrown.edu
admission@morrisbrown.edu

Paine College
800-476-7703
www.paine.edu
simpkins@mail.paine.edu

Savannah State College
912-356-2181
www.savstate.edu
SSUAdmissions@savstate.edu

Spelman College
800-982-2411
www.spelman.edu
admiss@spelman.edu

KENTUCKY

Kentucky State University
502-597-6813
www.kysu.edu
jburrell@gwmail.kysu.edu

LOUISIANA

Dillard University
504-816-4670
www.dillard.edu

Grambling State University
318-247-3811
www.gram.edu
bingamann@medgar.gram.edu

Southern University A and M College
225-771-2430
subr.edu
admit@subr.edu

Southern University—New Orleans
504-286-5314
www.suno.edu

Southern University—Shreveport
318-674-3300
www.susla.edu
info@susla.edu

Xavier University
504-483-7388
www.xula.edu
apply@xula.edu

MARYLAND

Bowie State University
301-464-6570
www.bowiestate.edu
kgolding@bowiestate.edu

Coppin State College
410-951-3600
www.coppin.edu
lthorton@wye.coppin.edu

Morgan State University
800-332-6674
www.morgan.edu
tjenness@moac.morgan.edu

University of Maryland—Eastern Shore
410-651-6410
www.umes.edu
ccmills@mail.umes.edu

MICHIGAN

Lewis College of Business
304-696-2314
lcob.marshall.edu
busley@marshall.edu

MISSISSIPPI

Alcorn State University
601-877-6147
www.alcorn.edu
nboyd@lorman.alcorn.edu

Coahoma Junior College
662-627-2571
www.ccc.cc.ms.us

Hinds Junior College—Utica Campus
800-HINDSCC
www.hindscc.edu
info@hindscc.edu

Jackson State University
601-979-2100
www.jsums.edu
schatman@ccaix.jsums.edu

Mary Holmes College
662-495-5100
www.maryholmes.edu
mhcinfo@maryholmes.edu

Mississippi Valley State University
662-254-3344
www.mvsu.edu
leewilson@mvsu.edu

Rust College
662-252-8000
www.rustcollege.edu
jbmcdonald@rustcollege.edu

Tougaloo College
888-424-2566
tougaloo.edu
slaterJa@mail.tougaloo.edu

Missouri

Harris–Stowe State College
314-340-3366
www.hssc.edu
admissions@hssc.edu

Lincoln University
573-681-5599
www.lincolnu.edu
enroll@lincolnu.edu

North Carolina

Barber–Scotia College
704-789-2901
www.barber-scotia.edu
wwhite@b-sc.edu

Bennett College
910-370-8624
www.bennett.edu
admiss@bennett1.bennett.edu

Elizabeth City State University
252-335-3305
www.ecsu.edu
admissions@mail.ecsu.edu

Fayetteville State University
910-486-1371
www.uncfsu.edu
cad@adm1.uncfsu.edu

Johnson C. Smith University
704-378-1011
www.jcsu.edu

Livingstone College
704-797-1000
www.livingstone.edu

North Carolina A and T State University
336-334-7946
www.ncat.edu
uadmit@ncat.edu

North Carolina Central University
919-560-6298
www.nccu.edu
ebridges@wpo.nccu.edu

St. Augustine's College
919-516-4016
www.st-aug.edu
admissions@es.st-aug.edu

Shaw University
919-546-8275
www.shawuniversity.edu
admission@shawu.edu

Winston–Salem State University
336-750-2070
www.wssu.edu
admissions@wssu1.adp.wssu.edu

OHIO

Central State University
937-376-6348
www.centralstate.edu
admissions@csu.ces.edu

Wilberforce University
800-376-8568
www.wilberforce.edu
kchristm@shorter.wilberforce

OKLAHOMA

Langston University
405-466-2231
www.lunet.edu
admission@speedy.lunet.edu

PENNSYLVANIA

Cheyney State University
610-399-2275
www.cheyney.edu
wbickley@cheyney.edu

Lincoln University
610-932-8300
www.lincoln.edu
admiss@lu.lincoln.edu

SOUTH CAROLINA

Allen University
803-376-5703
www.allenuniversity.edu
admissions@allenuniversity.edu

Benedict College
803-253-5143
www.bchome.benedict.edu
admission@benedict.edu

Claflin University
803-535-5339
www.claflin.edu
zeiglerm@clafl.claflin.edu

Denmark Technical College
803-793-5197
www.den.tec.sc.us

Morris College
803-934-3225
www.morris.edu
gscriven@morris.edu

South Carolina State University
800-260-5956
www.scsu.edu

Voorhees College
803-703-7111
www.voorhees.edu
elfphi@voorhees.edu

TENNESSEE

Fisk University
615-329-8666
www.fisk.edu
admissions@fisk.edu

Lane College
731-426-7532
www.lanecollege.edu
admissions@lanecollege.edu

LeMoyne–Owen College
800-737-7778
www.lemoyne-owen.edu/

Tennessee State University
615-963-3101
www.tnstate.edu
jcade@tnstate.edu

Huston–Tillotson College
512-505-3000
www.htc.edu

Jarvis Christian College
903-769-5730
www.jarvis.edu
colemana@jarvis.edu

Paul Quinn College
214-302-3648
www.pqc.edu

Prairie View A and M University
936-857-2626
www.pvamu.edu
mary_gooch@pvamu.edu

Saint Philip's College
210 531-4833
www.accd.edu

Southwestern Christian College
972-524-3341
www.swcc.edu

Texas College
903-593-8311
www.texascollege.edu
afrancis@texacollege.edu

Texas Southern University
713-313-7420
www.tsu.edu
thomas_gb@tsu.edu

Wiley College
903-927-3311
www.wileyc.edu
admissions@wileynrts.wileyc.edu

Virginia

Hampton University
757-727-5328
www.hamptonu.edu
webmaster@hamptonu.edu

Norfolk State University
757-823-8396
www.nsu.edu
admissions@nsu.edu

Saint Paul's College
434-848-4268
www.saintpauls.edu
admissions@saintpauls.edu

Virginia State University
804-524-5902
www.vsu.edu
vsuadm@vsu.edu

Virginia Union University
804-257-5881
www.vuu.edu
admissions@vuu.edu

West Virginia

Bluefield State College
540-326-4214
www.bluefield.edu
thavens@mail.bluefield.edu

West Virginia State College
800-987-2112
www.wvsc.edu
byersrc@oscar.wvsc.edu

U.S. Virgin Islands

University of the Virgin Islands
340-693-1150
www.uvi.edu
admissions@uvi.edu

INDEX OF STATE FINANCIAL AID OFFICES

Alabama
Commission on Higher Education
3465 Norman Ridge Rd.
Montgomery, AL 36105
334-281-1998
www.ache.state.al.us/

Alaska
Commission on Post Secondary Education
3030 Vintage Blvd.
Juneau, AK 99801
907-465-2967
www.stateak.us/acpe/

Arizona
Commission for Post Secondary Education
2020 N. Central Ave., #275
Pheonix, AZ 85004
602-229-2531
www.acpe.asu.edu

Arkansas
Department of Higher Education
114 E. Capitol St.
Little Rock, AR 72201
501-324-9300
www.adhe.arknet.edu/

California
Student Aid Commission
PO Box 419026
Rancho Cordova, CA 95741
916-526-7590
www.csac.ca.gov/

Colorado
Commission on Higher Education
1300 Broadway, 2nd Floor
Denver, CO 80203
303-866-2723
www.state.co.us/cche_dir/hecche.html

Connecticut
Department of Higher Education
61 Woodland St.
Hartford, CT 06105
860-947-1855
www.ctdhe.org

Delaware
Higher Education Commission
820 N. French St.
Wilmington, DE 19801
302-577-3240
www.doe.state.de.us/high-ed/

District of Columbia
Post Secondary Education Office
2100 M. L. King Jr. Ave., SE #401
Washington, DC 20020
202-727-3865
www.etown.edu/finaid/ProspectiveStudents/stategrants.htm

Florida
Student Financial Assistance
325 W. Gaines St.
Tallahassee, FL 32399
904-487-0649
www.free-4u.com/
   florida_student_financial_assistance_commission.htm

Georgia
Student Finance Authority
2082 E. Exchange Pl., #245
Tucker, GA 30084
770-414-3018
www.gsfc.org

Hawaii
Post Secondary Education Commission
Bachman Hall, Room 202
2444 Dole St.
Honolulu, HI 96822
808-956-8213
www.etown.edu/finaid/ProspectiveStudents/stategrants.htm

Idaho
State Board of Education
PO Box 83720
Boise, ID 83720
208-334-2270
www.idahoachieves.com

Illinois
Student Assistance Commission
1755 Lake Cook Rd.
Deerfield, IL 60015
847-948-8500
www.isac1.org/ilaid/ilaid.html

Indiana
Student Assistance Commission
150 West Market St., 5th Floor
Indianapolis, IN 46204
317-232-2350
www.in.gov/ssaci/programs/html

Iowa
Iowa College Aid Commission
914 Grand Ave., @201
Des Moines, IA 50309
515-281-3501
www.state.ia.us/collegeaid

Kansas
Board of Regents
700 SW Harrison, #1410
Topeka, KS 66603
785-296-3517
www.kansasregents.org/

Kentucky
Higher Education Assistance Authority
1050 U.S. 127 South #102
Frankfort, KY 40601-4323
502-696-7200
www.kheaa.com

Louisiana
Student Financial Assistance Commission
PO Box 91202
Baton Rouge, LA 70821-9202
504-922-1011, 800-259-5626
www.osfa.state.la.us/

Maine
Finance Authority of Maine
PO Box 949
Augusta, ME 04330
207-287-2183
www.famemaine.com

Maryland
Higher Education Commission
16 Francis St.
Annapolis, MD 21401
410-974-5370
www.mhec.state.md.us

Massachusetts
Higher Education Coordination Council
330 Stuart St.
Boston, MA 02116
617-727-9420
www.rushu.rush.edu/finaid/state.html

Michigan
Higher Education Assistance Authority
PO Box 30462
Lansing, MI 48909
517-373-3394
www.michigan.gov/mistudentaid

Minnesota
Higher Education Services Office
550 Cedar St., #400
St. Paul, MN 55101
612-296-3974
www.mheso.state.ms.us/

Missouri
Student Assistance Resource Services
3515 Amazonas Dr.
Jefferson City, MO 65102
574-751-3940
www.cbhe.state.mo.us/MOSTARS/mostars.htm

Mississippi
Financial Assistance Board
3825 Ridgewood Rd.
Jackson, MS 39211-6453
601-982-6663
www.esfweb.com/mheac.html

Montana
Montana University System
2500 Broadway
Helena, MT 5962-0
406-444-6594
www.montana.edu/mus/

Nebraska
Post Secondary Education Commission
PO Box 95005
Lincoln, NE 68509
402-471-6506
www.state.ne.us/NEpostsecondaryed/

Nevada
State Department of Education
400 W. King St.
Carson City, NV 89710
702-687-5915
www.nde.state.nv

New Hampshire
Post Secondary Education Commission
2 Industrial Park Dr.
Concord, NH 033011-8512
603-296-3974
www.state.nh.us/postsecondary/sfahelp.ed.gov/Link1.cfm

New Jersey
Office of State Financial Assistance
4 Quakerbridge Plaza, CN 540
Trenton, NJ 08625
609-588-3268, 800-792-8670
www.nmche.org

New Mexico
Commission on Higher Education
1068 Cerrillos Rd.
Santa Fe, NM 87501
505-827-7383
www.hesc.com

North Carolina
State Education Assistance Authority
PO Box 2988
Chapel Hill, NC 27515
919-549-8614
www.ncseaa.edu/

North Dakota
Student Financial Assistance Program
600 East Boulevard Ave.
Bismark, ND 58505
701-224-2271
www.free-4u.com/student_financial_assistance_program.htm

Ohio
Student Aid Commission
PO Box 182452
Columbus, OH 43218-2452
614-466-7420, 800-837-6752
www.state.oh.us/slc/

Oklahoma
State Regents for Higher Education
PO Box 3000
Oklahoma City, OK 73101
405-858-4300
www.okhighered.org/

Oregon
State Scholarship Commission
1500 Valley River Dr., #100
Eugene, OR 97401
541-687-7400
www.osac.state.or.us/

Pennsylvania
Higher Education Assistance Agency
1200 North 7th St.
Harrisburg, PA 17102
717-257-2800, 800-692-7435
www.free-4u.com/
    pennsilvania_higher_education_assistance_agency.htm

Rhode Island
Higher Education Assistance Authority
560 Jefferson Blvd.
Warwick, RI 02886
401-736-1100, 800-922-9855
www.riheaa.org

South Carolina
Higher Education Tuition Grants Commission
1310 Lady St., #811
Columbia, SC 29201
803-737-1200
www.sctuitiongrants.com/

South Dakota
Office of the Secretary, Department of Education
700 Governors Dr.
Pierre, SD 57501-2291
605-773-3134
www.nochildleftbehind.gov/next/where/southdakota.html

Tennessee
Tennessee Student Assistance Corporation
404 James Robertson Pkwy.
Parkway Towers, Suite 1900
Nashville, TN 37243-0820
615-741-3605, 800-342-1663
www.tsac.state.tn.us.master.com/texis/master/search

Texas
Higher Education Coordination Board
Box 12788, Capitol Station
Austin, TX 78711
512-483-6340, 800-242-3062
www.thecb.state.tx.us/

Utah
Utah State Board of Regents
335 W.N. Temple
2 Triad, #550
Salt Lake City, UT 84180
801-321-7205
www.utahsbr.edu

Vermont
Student Assistance Corporation
Champlain Mill, Box 2000
Winooski, VT 05404
802-655-9602, 800-642-3177
www.vsac.org

Virginia
Council of Higher Education
101 North 14th St.
Richmond, VA 23219
804-225-3146
www.ed.gov/Programs/bastmp/SHEA.htm

Washington
Higher Education Coordination Board
917 Lake Ridge Way, SW
Olympia, WA 98504
360-753-7800
www.hecb.wa.gov/

West Virginia
State Department of Education
1900 Washington St., #358
Charleston, WV 25305
304-588-2691
www.wvde.state.wv.us/

Wisconsin
Higher Education Aids Board
PO Box 7885
Madison, WI 53707
608-266-2354
www.witechcolleges.com/fin_aid.htm

Wyoming
State Department of Education
2300 Capitol Ave., 2nd Floor
Cheyenne, WY 82002
307-777-6265
www.k12.wy.us/index.htm

Guam
University of Guam
303 University Dr.
Mangilao, Guam 96923
www.uog.edu/

Saipan, Northern Mariana Islands
Northern Mariana Islands
PO Box 1250
670-234-5498
www.prel.org/pacserv/mariana.asp

Puerto Rico
PO Box 23305, UPR Station
Rio Piedras, PR 00931
www.ed.gov/Programs/bastme/SHEA.htm

Virgin Islands
PO Box 11900
St. Thomas, VI 00801
www.ed.gov/Programs/bastme/SHEA.htm

SCHOOL SAYS . . .

In this section you'll find profiles of schools describing their admissions standards, curriculum, internship opportunities, and much more. The Princeton Review charges each institution a small fee to be listed, and the editorial responsibility is solely that of the school.

BENTLEY COLLEGE

GENERAL INFORMATION

As a business university, Bentley College has the resources to invest in the tools of the information age, put them in student's hands, and offer a remarkable depth of business-related majors and concentrations. Bentley blends the breadth and technological strength of a university with the values and student orientation of a small college. The Bentley academic experience combines a strong arts and sciences foundation with the most advanced business education possible. This combination prepares students for success in our global, information-driven world. In courses and projects, students gain a solid understanding of technologies and have the opportunity to watch them come alive in several hands-on, high-tech learning laboratories—each among the first of its kind in higher education. In addition, through internships, jobs, campus activities, and study abroad opportunities, students gain the critical skills necessary to manage and analyze the nearly limitless amount of information that drives the business world.

Bentley enrolls approximately 4,250 full-time and part-time undergraduates. Students come from 40 U.S. states and more than 80 countries. On-campus housing options include single-, double-, or triple-occupancy dorm rooms; apartments; or suites. There are 13 residence halls and apartment-style buildings on campus, housing 78 percent of Bentley students.

Bentley's small-college environment delivers plenty of opportunities for fun. Students can explore current interests or develop new ones by getting involved in a wide range of on-campus activities, including athletic events, music and theater programs, and more than 70 clubs and student organizations. A new Student Center, opened in January 2002, is the heart of action outside the classroom. Students enjoy a large dining room, games room, The 1917 Tavern, campus radio station and newspaper, and office and meeting space for student organizations.

Bentley fields more than 23 varsity sports teams, which compete at the NCAA Division I and II levels. The College is a member of the Northeast-10 Conference, and the Division I Metro Atlantic Athletic Conference Hockey League. Many teams have regularly qualified for postseason competition, and individual athletes have routinely earned honors. Recreational athletes may take part in Bentley's ever-growing list of intramural sports and activities that include dance and fitness training.

Student athletes compete on brand new baseball and soccer fields, along with a state-of-the-art outdoor track and six new tennis courts. The Dana Athletic Center has all the resources needed for recreational athletes, including an indoor track, volleyball and racquetball courts, a competition-size indoor pool and diving tank, a weight room, and other facilities.

COSTS

Tuition in 2002–2003 is $22,965. Room and board (double room plus meal plan) costs $9,350. Additional costs include books, supplies, laptop computer, and personal and travel expenses.

ACADEMICS

Bentley combines the powerful resources of a business university with the strengths of a small college to help students develop the skills that employers are looking for. Students draw on a varied curriculum to shape an academic program that reflects their interests and goals.

Students learn to use information technology the way business does, as an important tool for planning, producing, marketing, and managing. Through the Mobile Computing Program all Bentley freshman receive a laptop that's network-ready and fully loaded with software. With computer ports located all over campus—classrooms, dining halls, dorm rooms and the library—students have incredibly fast and convenient access to the Internet, Bentley network, and many other information sources.

"Learn by doing" is a core philosophy at Bentley. Hands-on experience is a key to many courses and projects. Students get the opportunity to test drive concepts and theories learned in the classroom by working in one of Bentley's specialized learning labs, which include the financial Trading Room, Center for Marketing Technology, Accounting Lab, or Design and Usability Testing Center. Students also apply classroom theory to real-life situations through hands-on experiences such as internships, group consulting projects, service learning assignments, and other opportunities.

Bentley's service-learning program has consistently been recognized for leadership in the field of student character development. Recently, *U.S. News & World Report America's Best College 2003* ranked Bentley's Service-Learning Center number 10 nationwide. The Service Learning Center helps students build valuable skills in business, communication, and teamwork while also contributing to society.

Through aggressive on-campus recruiting, an online job listing service, an alumni database, career fairs, and workshops, the Miller Center for Career Services helps students explore career options, gain hands-on work experience, and connect with top employers. Within six months of graduation, about 93 percent of students find professional employment or enroll in graduate school full time.

An internship program allows students to fine-tune skills, explore interests, and make job connections, all while earning course credit. The program offers many opportunities at some of the leading companies in the U.S. Past internship positions have included organizations such as IBM, Reebok International, Big Five accounting firms, and Hewlett-Packard.

While focused on business, a Bentley education is broad in scope. Students have many options for creating an academic program that meets their needs and interests. Degree options include:

Bachelor of Science:

Accountancy, accounting information systems, computer information systems, corporate finance and accounting, economics-finance, finance, information design and corporate communication, management, managerial economics, marketing, and mathematical sciences.

Bachelor of Arts:

English, history, international studies, liberal arts, philosophy and public policy, and social change.

In addition, students can choose a BA in mathematics or design their own arts and sciences concentration in areas such as behavioral sciences, communication, or environmental studies.

Students can combine their interests by choosing a minor or concentration that complements their major area of study. Students also have the opportunity to apply to a special program that allows them to earn a bachelor's degree and a master's degree in five years.

Bentley follows the teacher-scholar model. Classes are not taught by teaching assistants or graduate assistants. Faculty members stay closely connected to the business world and interject real-life perspectives into classroom lectures and projects. With an average class size of 25 to 30 and a student/faculty ratio of 14:1, students benefit from a collaborative approach to teaching. There are 422 full-time and part-time faculty members; 82 percent of full-time professors hold doctoral degrees.

CAMPUS LIFE

Bentley is located 10 miles west of Boston, in Waltham, Massachusetts. Situated on 163 acres, the suburban campus represents the best of New England college campuses and provides an inviting atmosphere for study and socializing. The city's many resources are within easy reach; the Bentley shuttle makes regular trips to Harvard Square in Cambridge. From theater to art exhibits, dance clubs to alternative rock concerts, championship sports to championship shopping, Boston has the proverbial "something for everyone."

Bentley students can choose to spend a semester or entire year abroad in various countries including Australia, Belgium, England, France, Italy, and Spain. In addition, a cross-registration program allows students to enroll at nearby Brandeis University, Regis College, or the Wentworth Institute of Technology to take courses not currently offered at Bentley.

ADMISSIONS

Admission to Bentley is selective and is based on past accomplishments and future potential. Along with the application, Bentley requires a secondary school transcript, letters of recommendation from a teacher and a counselor, and official results of either the SAT or ACT test. Prospective students are encouraged to complete a solid college-preparatory program, which includes 4 years of English, 4 years of mathematics (preferably algebra I and II, geometry, and a senior-year math course), and 3 to 4 years each of history, laboratory science, and foreign language.

For regular admission, students must submit all required documents by February 1 for September admission and by November 15 for January admission. Candidates are notified by April 1 for the fall semester and by December 5 for the spring semester.

Designed for academic achievers for whom Bentley is the first choice, the Early Decision program allows for an admission decision by January 1. If admitted, candidates must withdraw any applications to other colleges. Students may also participate in the Early Action program if Bentley is among their top choices but they prefer not to make a commitment in January. The application deadline for both programs is December 1. Bentley College also accepts the Common Application.

All international students must file an international student application. Applicants who are non-native speakers of English must also have official results of the Test of English as a Foreign Language (TOEFL) forwarded to the Office of Undergraduate Admission.

For additional information, students should contact:

Office of Undergraduate Admission
Bentley College
175 Forest Street
Waltham, MA 02452-4705
Telephone: 781-891-2244, 800-523-2354
Fax: 781-891-3414
E-mail: ugadmission@bentley.edu
World Wide Web: www.bentley.edu

FISK UNIVERSITY

COLLEGE AT A GLANCE

From its founding in 1866, Fisk University in Nashville, Tennessee, has been one of America's outstanding universities, providing an exceptional liberal arts education. Fisk graduates have a mastery of critical thinking skills and are well read in the humanities, the social sciences, and the physical and natural sciences. A Fisk education produces men and women who are independent thinkers and who are able to assume leadership positions at the highest levels of society.

Attendance at Fisk University provides the opportunity to work with first-rate faculty members whose scholarship, classroom instruction, and dedication to the liberal arts have earned them worldwide recognition. Students experience individualized professorial assistance in a small, personalized classroom environment.

HISTORY

From its earliest days, Fisk has played a leadership role in the education of African Americans. Fisk students, faculty, and alumni have been among America's intellectual, artistic, and civic leaders in every generation since the University's founding. The tradition of excellence at Fisk began with Fisk students. Fisk's world-famous Jubilee Singers introduced much of the world to the spiritual as a musical genre, and in the process raised funds that permitted construction of Jubilee Hall, the South's first permanent structure built for the education of black students. W.E.B. Du Bois (Fisk class of 1888), the great social critic and co-founder of the NAACP, was an early illustrious alumnus of the university. Distinguished artist Aaron Douglas served on the Fisk faculty for many years, and his murals decorate the walls of the university's administration building. Arna Bontemps, Sterling A. Brown, Robert Hayden, and James Weldon Johnson were among the Fisk faculty members who became major figures in American literature. Probably no single institution has played so central a role as Fisk in the shaping of African American learning and culture in America.

LEADERSHIP

The Fisk liberal arts tradition continues to provide students with the broad humanistic perspective that good leaders must have. Students can enjoy the Carl Van Vechten Gallery, which houses a truly outstanding collection, including works by 29 prominent modernists such as Picasso, Cézanne, Renoir, O'Keefe, and Toulouse-Lautrec. The Aaron Douglas Gallery features an equally outstanding collection of works by African-American artists such as Tanner, Douglas, Lawrence, Bearden, Driskell, and Ridley. In marked contrast, but consistent with its liberal arts tradition, the university also houses the NASA Center for Photonic Materials and Devices and the Fisk Infrared Spectroscopy Institute, where students can work with the university's award-winning physicists. The Fisk University Library and Media Center contain some of the oldest and most definitive collections of African-American history and culture, including such rare items as the Bible presented to President Lincoln by free blacks in 1864; the first edition of Phyllis Wheatley's *Poems on Various Subjects* (1773); and papers belonging to W.E.B. Du Bois, Aaron Douglas, and Langston Hughes.

ACADEMIC PROGRAMS

Business Administration: Accounting, business administration, financial economics, international business relations, management

Humanities and Fine Arts: Art, dance, dramatics and speech, English, mass communications, modern foreign languages, music, religion and philosophical studies

Natural Sciences and Mathematics: Biology, chemistry, computer science, mathematics, physics, dual degree program—engineering, dual degree program—pre-pharmacy

Social Sciences: History, political science, psychology, sociology, teacher education

CAMPUS LIFE AT FISK

Fisk's reputation is built on high standards in scholarship, on a serious approach to study, and on an insistence on clear thinking and effective writing and speaking. The student's first obligation is to carefully and thoroughly do the work associated with academic courses. The faculty recognizes that some of the most important learning of the college years may come about through voluntary activities outside the classroom, particularly such activities as debating, editing of student publications, membership in the choir, and other pastimes that engage and stretch the student's critical intelligence, appreciation for the arts, and capability for collaborative work with others. Invaluable qualities of character, initiative, imagination, responsibility, and judgment may develop from such experiences, and the faculty therefore recognizes such experiences as an indispensable part of a college education, even though they are not always represented within the formal academic curriculum.

Students are encouraged to attend the cultural programs presented on the campus, including music recitals, showings of outstanding films, and lectures and discussions on literature and the arts and on national and international affairs. They are also encouraged to participate in the student government of the University and in campus organizations directed by students. By assuming responsibility in these phases of university life, students can obtain the training necessary for good citizenship and effective leadership. The best training for mature citizenship in town, state, and nation is active citizenship as a member of the University community.

FAST FACTS

Institutional control: Private nonprofit

Religious affiliation: None

Campus size: 40 acres

Setting: Located in a major urban area

Number of undergraduate students: 845

Number of graduate students: 36

Admissions office:

Mr. William Carter
Phone: 615-329-8665
Fax: 615-329-8774
E-mail: admit@fisk.edu

Financial aid office:

Mr. Mark Adkins
Phone: 615-329-8735
Fax: 615-329-8774
E-mail: madkins@fisk.edu

Cost of attendance:

Undergraduate tuition (full year): $10,400

Typical room charge (full year): $3,100

Typical board charge (full year): $2,240

Organizations:

Number of registered organizations: 71

Number of honor societies: 9

Number of social fraternities: 4

Number of social sororities: 4

Majors: Psychology and Education

ADMISSION REQUIREMENTS

Fisk University seeks to enroll men and women who will benefit from a liberal arts experience designed to equip them for intellectual and social leadership. It is the policy of Fisk University to grant admission to applicants showing evidence of adequate preparation and the ability to successfully pursue college studies at Fisk University.

Applicants for admission to the freshman class should fulfill the following requirements:

1. Graduate from an accredited secondary school with a scholastic record that predicts success at a liberal arts college such as Fisk.

2. Present a minimum of 15 acceptable units of high school credits properly distributed in curriculum.

3. Have competitive SAT and ACT scores.

4. Have a minimum grade point average of 2.5 (on a 4.0 scale).

5. Have strong endorsements from their principal, headmaster, counselor, or teacher in regard to their academic ability, motivation, character, citizenship, and leadership qualities.

Formal application for admission to Fisk is normally made between September 1 and June 15 of the senior year. Application for admission to the second term should be completed by November 1.

Cost and value are important to everyone these days. By all standards, Fisk University is an exceptionally good buy in higher education. For five consecutive years we have been on *Money* magazine's list of "best values in education," which is based on the quality of education in relationship to the cost. This year we were ranked 18th among all public and private colleges and universities in the United States, as well as the nation's most affordable historically black university.

Fisk believes that if you've worked hard enough to qualify for admission to our university, you should be able to study here—regardless of your family's economic status. And we'll work with you to make sure that it's possible. More than 85 percent of our students are receiving financial aid in the form of grants, scholarships, loans, or work-study.

Types of aid offered at Fisk are both campus-based and non-campus-based. With few exceptions, financial aid is awarded for an academic year, which, although not automatic, is renewable by application on a yearly basis. So students who enter Fisk with financial assistance will normally be able to renew it as long as they continue to meet applicable university and federal requirements.

Due to the competitiveness for scholarships and financial aid, students are encouraged to complete the Application for Undergraduate Admission kit and submit it to the financial aid office as early as possible. Although the deadline for consideration is April 20, we recommend that students submit their applications at the same time they apply for admission to Fisk.

To be considered for any type of financial aid, tuition remission, or academic scholarship, applicants must complete the Free Application for Federal Student Aid (FAFSA) and submit it to the Federal Processor in Iowa City, Iowa.

VISIT CAMPUS

Prospective students may visit campus at any time. By calling the Office of Admission at 615-329-8665, they can also arrange a detailed tour and classroom visit and experience Fisk as current students do. Visit us on the Web at www.fisk.edu and enter into the admission page to log on to a live chat with current students and counselors.

NORTHEASTERN UNIVERSITY

AT A GLANCE

Northeastern University was founded in 1898 to serve Boston's emerging working-class and immigrant communities. The University has always drawn strength from its urban environment, which includes great libraries and research institutions, powerful engines of commerce and technology, and most important, diverse people and cultures whose ideas and perspectives enrich the experiences of its students.

Northeastern is creating the kind of supportive, pluralistic community that can serve as a national model. The University is nationally recognized for its academic excellence and its diverse community: more than 20 percent of our students are people of color, and students come here from all 50 states and 113 countries. Students who join our community benefit from a rich variety of programs that support them academically, culturally, and socially. Consider a few examples:

- The John D. O'Bryant African-American Institute, which has provided a home away from home for students of color for 30 years
- Programs in the College of Arts and Sciences that enable students to major in African American studies and minor in Latino, Latin American, and Caribbean studies
- The Program in Multicultural Engineering, which assists engineering students from all backgrounds
- Lectures, seminars, and roundtables that give students the opportunity to share ideas with distinguished visitors such as *Washington Week in Review* host Gwen Ifill, civil rights activist Dick Gregory, and President Clinton's special counsel Christopher Edley

CAMPUS AND LOCATION

Northeastern truly offers students the best of both worlds. The 66-acre campus is traditional, with well-manicured open spaces, a full range of student services, and modern residence halls and academic buildings. However, the campus is in the heart of Boston, the ultimate college town. More than 300,000 students attend college in Boston, and Northeastern is just steps away from the city's cultural, educational, and recreational riches. Three stops on Boston's subway system, the "T," are located on campus, giving students easy and affordable access to the entire city. Northeastern is located on Huntington Avenue, the "Avenue of the Arts," putting it within walking distance many of the city's finest attractions, including the Museum of Fine Arts, where admission is free for Northeastern students; Symphony Hall; Fenway Park, home of Major League Baseball's Red Sox; and the Isabella Stuart Gardner Museum.

Students are guaranteed on-campus housing their first two years at Northeastern. Ninety percent of freshmen live on campus in 12 co-ed residence halls. Upperclass students can live in traditional residence halls or in one of Northeastern's newer apartment complexes, many of which offer spectacular Boston views.

DEGREES OFFERED

Northeastern has seven colleges and schools: the Colleges of Arts and Sciences, Business Administration, Computer Science, Criminal Justice, and Engineering; Bouvé College of Health Sciences; and the School of Engineering Technology. Collectively, these colleges offer 100 undergraduate majors and minors and 40 dual degree programs. Students also have the option of designing an interdisciplinary major to meet their own interests and goals.

PROGRAMS AND CURRICULUM

A Northeastern education is built on the idea that every form of learning—whether in the classroom, in the workplace, or in the community, is crucial to preparing students for their careers and their lives. The curriculum combines course work in the liberal arts and professional studies with a cooperative education (co-op) program and other types of hands-on learning to give students a comprehensive education.

Through co-op, students alternate classroom study with periods of full-time, paid work experience related to their majors or interests. The typical curriculum takes five years; however, a four-year option with fewer co-op periods is available in most programs.

OFF-CAMPUS OPPORTUNITIES

Northeastern encourages its students to explore the surrounding city, the country, and the world.

Northeastern offers an extensive study abroad program, in which about 250 students participate each year. There are study abroad programs in more than 40 countries, and a number of them include research projects, internships, and co-op jobs as well as traditional classroom study.

The co-op program is a means for students to explore other parts of the country and the world as well. As part of the unique bachelor's degree program in international business, students spend a year abroad studying and working a co-op job. Co-op jobs are available in 33 states, with Washington, D.C., and New York City being two popular destinations.

FACILITIES

Northeastern offers unmatched facilities for both learning and recreation. The Snell Library is the largest academic library in Boston with more than 1 million books, periodicals, electronic journals, and news sources, which students can access through the NUCAT online catalog system. The library also contains the InfoCommons, a 160-workstation computer lab, and the new CyberCafe, where students can grab a snack, mingle, and connect to the Internet.

The new Behrakis Health Sciences Center, opened in fall 2002, is the academic home for students in the Bouvé College of Health Sciences. The $37 million building includes clinical and simulation labs that are equipped with the latest technology for teaching and research. The Snell Engineering Center and the Egan Engineering/Science Research Center contain modern laboratories with telecommunications and computer-aided manufacturing equipment and multimedia rooms.

The Curry Student Center is the hub of social activity on campus. It contains offices for student clubs; meeting and function rooms; and a variety of services for students, including a food court, travel agency, hair salon, overnight delivery service facility, dry cleaner, florist, bookstore, and the new afterHOURs, a late-night club where students can dine, dance, watch television, and listen to music.

The Marino Recreation Center is a state-of-the-art, three-level fitness center with a suspended running track, basketball courts, a Treadwall that simulates rock climbing, a variety of cardiovascular equipment and weight machines, free weights, and exercise rooms.

TUITION, ROOM AND BOARD, AND FEES

For the 2002–2003 academic year, estimated tuition, room and board, and fees for freshmen were $32,490. Tuition for upperclassmen varies depending on the student's pattern of attendance. When students are on co-op, they do not pay tuition. They are, however, still considered full-time students and may continue to pay room and board to live in a campus residence hall while they are working.

Northeastern is committed to keeping the University affordable for all students. The University provides scholarships to two-thirds of its full-time undergraduates, including a number of merit scholarships for students of color. For the 2001–2002 academic year, 82 percent of students received some form of financial aid—usually a mix of scholarship, grant, loan, and work opportunities. The average freshman financial aid package was $15,348. The amount of financial aid varies based on financial need, the student's academic promise, and the availability of University funds.

Students applying for merit scholarships should submit their Northeastern applications by January 1 and their Free Application for Federal Student Aid (FAFSA) and the College Scholarship Service's CSS/Financial Aid PROFILE by February 15.

STUDENTS

Northeastern's student body of 13,963 is as diverse as the urban community that surrounds it. Students come to Northeastern from all 50 states and 113 countries, and 20 percent are students of color. More than 4,000 students are involved in campus organizations and more than 4,500 hundred participate in varsity, club, or intramural sports. Of the students admitted to the most recent class, 86 percent ranked in the top 50 percent of their high school graduating class.

ADMISSIONS

Admission to Northeastern is selective and competitive. Each year, more than 16,000 applicants apply for 2,800 places in the freshman class. In building a diverse and talented incoming class, Northeastern looks for applicants who have been successful academically and who have been involved in high school activities and their communities. Students who have earned strong grades in a rigorous college preparatory program, are innovative, and possess leadership abilities are most successful in our admission process.

For priority consideration, students are encouraged to submit their completed applications by February 15. January 1 is the deadline for students competing for merit-based scholarships. Applicants interested in physical therapy, visual arts, and music technology should apply before February 1. Students who apply by February 15 will be mailed a final decision by April 1. To apply, students should submit the following:

- Completed application and nonrefundable $50 application fee
- Secondary school transcripts including senior-year first-quarter grades
- Official SAT I or ACT results
- Teacher recommendation
- Guidance counselor recommendation
- Transcripts from any college-level course work
- Personal statement/essay
- Description of extracurricular activities and involvement
- Declaration of finances form (international students only)
- English language test results (for students whose primary language is not English)

Students may apply online at www.neu.edu/admission.

ADDITIONAL INFORMATION

Students wanting more information about Northeastern university should contact:

The Office of Undergraduate Admissions
Undergraduate Admissions Visitor Center
Northeastern University
30 Leon Street
Boston, MA 02115
617-373-2200 (voice)
617-373-2211 (tours and interviews)
617-373-8780 (fax)
617-373-3100 (TTY)
www.northeastern.edu/admissions
admissions@neu.edu

OLIN SCHOOL OF BUSINESS

GENERAL INFORMATION

At Olin, you'll find a supportive community where each person's interests and ideas make a difference. With approximately 160 MBA students in a class, you're assured of receiving individual attention from our faculty and staff. And it's likely that you'll get to know our dean, Stuart Greenbaum.

Olin's curriculum is based on the understanding that no two students are identical—therefore, no single, prescribed curriculum is expected to meet everyone's needs. That's what makes the Olin curriculum different: it's flexible, it's based on a relatively small set of required classes and a large number of electives, and it acknowledges students' individual strengths and career aspirations.

Experiential learning is an important element in your learning strategy. We offer a broad and innovative menu of hands-on learning opportunities that enable you to apply your classroom knowledge to real-life business situations. These programs help you develop confidence in your leadership ability, gain consulting experience, and hone your communication and teamwork skills.

CONSORTIUM FOR GRADUATE STUDY IN MANAGEMENT

The Consortium for Graduate Study in Management (CGSM) was cofounded by Olin 35 years ago to encourage enrollment of underrepresented minorities in graduate management programs. CGSM fellowships are made possible through school and corporate support and provide full tuition for MBA study at one of 14 participating schools. To apply for these competitive, merit-based awards, you must be an American citizen who belongs to one of the following minority groups: African American, Hispanic American, or Native American. Your CGSM application serves as your Olin application. For information, call the Consortium Office at 888-658-6814 or contact the office via e-mail at frontdesk@cgsm.org. Their Internet address is www.cgsm.org.

ADMISSIONS

Admission to Olin is selective. The Olin Admissions Committee reviews applications based on a series of four deadlines, with the earliest falling in mid-November. Qualified full-time MBA students are admitted to start in the fall semester only. The committee reviews all information in the application to determine a candidate's ability to perform in an intensely rigorous academic environment. The committee also seeks to identify students who will add significantly to the academic, cultural, and social character of the School. Prospective students must submit an Olin application in hard copy, online, or through MBA Multi-App interactive software. The committee also requires a current GMAT score, results of the TOEFL exam (if applicable), official transcripts from each university previously attended, a work history form, essays, a resume, and two letters of recommendation. Interviews are strongly encouraged.

ACADEMICS

For more information on the Olin experience at Washington University in St. Louis, visit our website at www.olin.wustl.edu.

The following degrees are offered:

- BSBA
- MSBA
- MBA (full-time)
- MBA (part-time)
- Executive degree programs
- PhD

Approximately 24 tenured professors, 30 additional tenure-track professors, 8 visiting professors, and 16 part-time professors who are world-class scholars serve on Olin's faculty. They hold positions on editorial boards, publish articles in top journals, and earn distinction as exemplary teachers and strong community builders who further the vision of the Olin School. They are instrumental in developing the curriculum to reflect state-of-the-art business practices. Twenty adjunct faculty members who are leaders in the business community bring to the classroom a passion for merging business theory with cutting-edge business practices.

CAMPUS LIFE

Founded in 1853, Washington University is recognized among the Top 20 universities in the United States according to *U.S. News & World Report*. The University is located in a picturesque suburban setting and is within walking distance of Forest Park. The Hilltop Campus, where Olin is situated, is seven miles west of the Mississippi Riverfront and the St. Louis Arch. Learning takes place in the supportive, comfortable atmosphere of a small college with the resources and amenities of a larger university. St. Louis is a thriving metropolitan center with notable art galleries, museums, theatre, sporting events, and bustling ethnic neighborhoods. It is home to a dynamic corporate community that fosters projects, internships, and mentoring programs for Olin MBAs.

John E. Simon Hall: Opened in 1986, the Olin School occupies John E. Simon Hall. The 80,000-square-foot building houses modern classrooms and study areas, an extensive library with online computer linkups to all major data systems, modern faculty and administrative offices, and a 70-unit computer lab for student use.

Charles F. Knight Executive Education Center: The Knight Center, Olin's new executive residential living and learning facility, reflects Washington University's tradition of world-class scholarship and research, as well as the Olin School's philosophy of education for a lifetime of achievement. The 135,000-square-foot building includes classrooms, breakout rooms, lounges, a dining area, 66 bedrooms, administrative offices, a fitness center, and a pub.

STUDENT BODY

The full-time MBA program enrolls approximately 150 new students each year. They have diverse undergraduate backgrounds ranging from business and the humanities to engineering and the sciences. On average, an entering class includes students from more than 30 states and as many as 26 foreign countries. Students also have the opportunity to participate in one or more of Olin's 15 student organizations. These organizations allow students to further expand their professional network and hone leadership skills. A student-administered honor code designed to govern full-time MBA students represents Olin MBAs' commitment to excellence in the classroom, and sends a direct message to future employers: students are graduating from a community that actively practices an exemplary standard of integrity.

SAM M. WALTON COLLEGE OF BUSINESS

AT A GLANCE

The University of Arkansas is rapidly carving out a reputation as one of America's rising star academic communities. A degree from the University of Arkansas will be associated with high academic quality no matter where you choose to live and work. Because of our affordability and the excellence of our students, faculty, staff, and facilities, the University of Arkansas was selected as one of America's 100 Best College Buys. In addition, our inclusion in *The Fiske Guide to College*, along with 294 other top public and private colleges and universities, places the University of Arkansas in the top 8 percent of the 4,048 institutions of higher learning in America.

This academic quality is apparent on many fronts. As *The Chronicle of Higher Education* pointed out in its September 14, 2001, issue, "Last year, when Harvard was shut out of the Rhodes and Yale was passed over for the Marshall, Arkansas won one of each."

The University of Arkansas is one of the nation's great public universities, in one of American's best college towns.

ACADEMICS

Students get much more than a school with a strong academic reputation when choosing the University of Arkansas. The U of A offers 219 academic programs from which you can find the major that is right for you. Yet, as research universities go, we are on the small, intimate side. That means smaller classes and more individual attention from faculty. A recent donation of $300 million from the Walton Foundation (the largest grant ever to any public university) contributes to the support of our Honors College, where students are supported in a very personalized fashion and encouraged to engage in scholarship and research with each other and the faculty.

STUDENTS

Ethnically, 12.3 percent of University of Arkansas students are U.S. minority students, and 5.8 percent are international. Total enrollment was 16,035 in the fall of 2002. In fall 2001, African American enrollment grew by 1.6 percent, from 965 to 980, and topped 1,000 in 2002.

Our students continue to excel at the national level. This past year, we had 48 students staking their claim to the nation's most prestigious scholarships and awards. These included a British Marshall Scholarship, a first team *USA Today* Academic All-American, two Barry Goldwater Scholarships, one Truman Scholarship, one Fulbright Scholarship, four National Science Foundation Graduate Fellowships, a James Madison Scholarship, and a David L. Boren Scholarship. We also had five finalists for the Rhodes Scholarship this past year, a tremendous achievement by any standard.

FACILITIES AND EQUIPMENT

E-mail and access to the Internet, including free dial-up accounts and space for Web page development, are available to all students, faculty, and staff. Also, 90 percent of campus residence halls are wired for high-speed, direct network access. Networked servers provide access to word processing, spreadsheet, database, graphics, and statistical package applications. Students have access to more than 1,400 PCs, Macs, and Unix workstations through numerous general purpose and special purpose computer labs located throughout the campus.

We are planning $642 million in new buildings and improvements over the remainder of the decade. As you look around our campus, you will see that some of this is underway. In the North Quadrant of campus, we will soon begin construction of a new 600-bed student residence hall complex. This $46 million project is scheduled to be completed by summer 2004. Over the last two years, the Science and Engineering Building has been totally renovated, at a cost of $11 million.

CAMPUS AND LOCATION

The University of Arkansas campus proper comprises 130 buildings on 345 acres. It rests upon a hilltop that overlooks the Ozark Mountains to the south. Old Main, the campus signature building, is one of 11 campus buildings that have been placed on the National Register of Historic Places.

The campus also is graced by the unique, much-loved tradition of Senior Walk. Since the University's founding, the names of all of its 115,000 graduates have been etched into more than five miles of campus sidewalks, their names arranged by year of graduation.

The University's home town, Fayetteville, is situated on the beautiful Ozark plateau, with friendly people, safe streets, a moderate climate, racial and ethnic diversity, awesome recreational opportunities, a robust economy, a vibrant cultural life, and all of the excitement you would expect from a great college town. Fayetteville is one of only 23 locales and the only Arkansas location to be included in the book *The Most Beautiful Villages and Towns of the South*.

COST AND FINANCIAL AID

The U of A awards over $2 million in scholarships to new students each academic year. The application for admission serves as the application for scholarships for the majority of scholarships offered to students by the University of Arkansas. Each new freshman who submits his or her application for admission and supporting documentation by February 15 will receive scholarship consideration.

Tuition, fees, room, and board average $8,748 for in-state students and $14,030 for most out-of-state students. For details regarding what your costs might be, we encourage you to contact the financial aid or scholarship office.

Aside from $49.4 million made available to UA undergraduates in federal grants-in-aid, loans, and work-study funds, the University makes $33.9 million available in institutionally and privately funded scholarship programs awarded on a competitive basis.

VISIT

Contact us online (admission.uark.edu) and set up a time to visit the UA campus. You can also schedule your visit by phone (800-377-8632 or 501-575-5346) or fax (501-575-7515). While you are here, take a tour, talk to professors, chat with students, have lunch, sit in on a class, meet with an admission counselor, and find out about scholarships and financial aid. Also, explore your special interests, such as band, orchestra, or athletics. Learn about campus life, activities, and organizations.

ADMISSION

Your admission to the U of A depends on your grade point average, class rank, ACT or SAT scores, personal essay, and evidence of commitment and desire to succeed. All new freshmen and those transfer students with fewer than 24 transferable semester hours need to evaluate their core courses to make sure they have 4 years of English, 3 years of mathematics, 3 years of social science, 3 years of science, and 3 college preparatory electives. The application for admission is due by February 15.

EXTRACURRICULAR ACTIVITIES AND CAMPUS LIFE

University Programs, also known as UP, is a student-run organization that plans, organizes, and promotes more than 300 events every year. UP depends on student volunteers to serve on its eight different committees. These committees are lead by committee chairs, who work with the president, vice president, public relations coordinator, gallery coordinator, and staff advisors to achieve the overall goal of bringing exciting, unique, fun, and educational events to the University of Arkansas campus. It all starts and ends with *you*, the student!

The University offers a vibrant campus life for its mainly full-time, residential undergraduate student population. University residence halls accommodate approximately 3,200 students, and the rest live in and about the city of Fayetteville.

Students have 263 registered student organizations at their disposal, including special interest organizations, religious organizations, international and cultural organizations, honorary and professional service organizations, student government, and more. Greek life is robust as well; in 2000–2001, 17 percent of male and 19 percent of female undergraduates belonged to the 22 fraternities and sororities on campus.

Culturally and intellectually, the academic semesters overflow with faculty and student musical performances, theatre productions, art exhibits, concerts, poetry readings, and visiting speakers—both on campus and at the adjacent Walton Arts Center. The Arkansas Union Society stirs lively student debate on topical issues several times a semester.

The Division of Student Affairs enhances the University of Arkansas experience by helping students to become intellectually engaged, more self-aware, and strongly bonded to the institution. Through its various departments—General Student Services, the Arkansas Union, University Health Services, Career Services, University Housing, and Special Projects and Services—the Division provides leadership in the development of programs and services that supplement the classroom experience, shape student leadership skills, and enrich the quality of campus life.

LEARNING DISABILITY

Adjusting to a university setting presents many challenges for new students, especially for those with disabilities. The University of Arkansas, Fayetteville, makes every effort to offer equal educational opportunities for all students and is committed to improving the total university experience for students with disabilities. The Center for Students with Disabilities (CSD) plays an important role in providing equal opportunities for students with disabilities and serves as a liaison among administrators, faculty, and students. The philosophy underlying the provision of services is one that maximizes each student's opportunities for success and helps students develop and maintain independence in college and beyond.

ST. JOHN FISHER COLLEGE

THE COLLEGE AT A GLANCE

Since its founding in 1948 by the Basilian Fathers, St. John Fisher College has remained devoted to the individual growth of each member of its student body. Initially a Catholic institution for men, today Fisher is both independent and coeducational. In fact, 59 percent of the students are female. Approximately half of the student body lives on campus. Students pursue undergraduate degrees in business, the humanities, nursing, the sciences, and the social sciences. Twelve graduate programs are offered as well. Fisher is an accredited member of the Middle States Association of Colleges and Schools.

The College offers a wide variety of extracurricular options to serve the multitude of interests held by its 2,100 full-time and 1,000 part-time students. For instance, students can choose from a campus newspaper, radio station, or television station. Or sign up for one of the many academic clubs. There are nearly 40 student organizations in all. The Student Activities Board regularly brings lectures and entertainment to campus. The FishBowl—Fisher's student union—is the location for many of these events.

Fisher competes in the NCAA Division III athletics, ECAC, and Empire 8. Intercollegiate men's teams include baseball, basketball, football, golf, lacrosse, soccer, and tennis. Intercollegiate women's teams include basketball, lacrosse, soccer, softball, tennis, cheerleading, and volleyball. Men's rugby and women's rugby are available as a club sport. At the Student Life Center, the heart of athletic life on campus, students can take advantage of basketball, racquetball, squash, tennis, and volleyball courts, in addition to a new fitness center. Growney Stadium—where the football, soccer, and lacrosse teams host their competition—boasts an all-season synthetic turf that permits teams to play in any weather, night or day. The 2,100-capacity stadium has bleacher seating and is topped with a press box. Other athletic features on campus include a recently constructed baseball complex, a softball field, a golf course with nine holes, and outside tennis courts. The Buffalo Bills hold their pre-season Training Camp at Fisher every summer.

STUDENTS

The Student Government Association—an organization that serves the judicial, as well as social and cultural, needs of the student body—fosters individual leadership skills. The Resident Student Association is elected by resident students and addresses issues germane to on-campus living. The Commuter Council is elected by commuting students.

ACADEMICS

To receive a bachelor's degree, students must complete at least 120 credit hours and achieve a final GPA of no lower than 2.0. At least 30 credit hours and 50 percent of requirements for a major must be completed at the College to earn a degree. Students graduating with an accounting degree are automatically eligible to take the CPA and CMA tests.

Fisher runs on a two-semester basis. During the summer, three sessions are held.

At St. John Fisher College, students can earn a Bachelor of Arts, Bachelor of Science, Master of Business Administration, Master of Science, and Master of Science in Education. Undergraduate programs are available in accounting, American studies, anthropology, biology, chemistry, childhood education, communication/journalism, computer science, economics, English, French, history, interdisciplinary studies, international studies, management, mathematics, math/science/technology education, nursing, philosophy, physics, political science, psychology, religious studies, sociology, Spanish, special education, and sport studies. Concentrations within the management program include finance, general business management, human resource management, and marketing.

With a full-time faculty count of 123, Fisher is able to provide an education centered on personal attention to students both inside and outside of the classroom. The 16:1 student/faculty ratio is a testament to this individual emphasis. Eighty-five percent of Fisher's full-time faculty has earned doctoral or equivalent degrees. Three-quarters of the College's classes have under 30 students. As students explore the opportunities in Fisher's 27 majors, they can take advantage of academic advising services offered through the Office of Academic Affairs and the College's dedicated faculty.

CAMPUS LIFE

Situated on a spacious 140-acre campus, St. John Fisher College combines the energy of the city with a sense of suburban calm. The campus is only a 10-minute drive from the heart of Rochester, a city regarded as the "World's Image Centre" and renowned as one of New York State's cultural centers. In Rochester, students can enjoy the Eastman Theater, the International Museum of Photography, the Rochester Museum and Science Center, the Rochester Philharmonic Orchestra, and the Strasenburgh Planetarium. And with a thriving professional life based around companies such as Bausch and Lomb, Eastman Kodak Company, and Xerox Corporation, Rochester provides a plethora of possibilities for student internships and post-graduation employment.

COSTS

Fisher is dedicated to providing assistance to each student in need. Fisher meets this challenge through a range of grants, scholarships, loans, and work-study offered through federal, state, and institutional sources. Financial aid awards averaged $ 14,400 per student in 2001–2002.

The College administers a merit-based academic scholarship. Students are assessed for these scholarships on the basis of high-school rank, GPA, and scores on the SAT I or ACT. The Office of Undergraduate Admissions reviews all applications for academic scholarship eligibility and notifies qualified students. Academic scholarship amounts begin at $4,500 for first-year students and $3,000 for transfers.

In 1996, Fisher began the Service Scholars Program, which acknowledges and rewards incoming students who have demonstrated a commitment to helping others through community service. This scholarship, which lasts all four years, covers one-third of the annual tuition, fees, and room and board costs. The John Templeton Foundation has twice named this program one of 60 exemplary programs in the Volunteer Service Programs Category.

Through the Fannie and Sam Constantino First Generation Scholarship Program, established in 1998, the College is able to offer assistance to first-generation college students. Awards range from a $4,500 scholarship to one-third of the annual tuition, fees, and room and board costs.

For the 2002–2003 academic year, tuition and fees total $16,400. Room and board, which includes a residence hall room and a meal plan, is $7,050.

ADMISSIONS

Applicants to St. John Fisher College are considered on the basis of high school GPA and rank, recommendations from high school faculty or officials, and results on the SAT I or ACT. While interviews are not required, they are highly encouraged.

To receive admission to St. John Fisher College, a candidate must have graduated from high school (or an acceptable equivalent) and completed at least 16 college-preparatory courses in a combination of the following fields: English, foreign languages, mathematics, natural sciences, and social sciences. An average grade of B or higher should have been earned in these courses.

Transfer students in good academic standing at two- and four-year institutions are welcome to apply for fall or spring admittance. Qualified transfer students will have an overall GPA of at least 2.0. Transfer student who have already completed an AA, AS, or AAS may transfer 60–66 credits. The Undergraduate Bulletin includes further details for transfer students.

Students with express academic or financial need may apply to participate in the NYS HEOP (Higher Education Opportunity Program), which seeks to help qualified students find academic achievement through scholastic support programs, individual counseling, and financial assistance.

Students who earn satisfactory results on Advanced Placement (AP) exams, the New York College Examination, and the College-Level Examination Program (CLEP) can receive academic course credit. To earn credit for AP exams, students must earn at least a 3 on all exams except the science and language exams, which require a 4.

Fisher adheres to a rolling admissions policy. For freshman applying for the fall semester, February 1 is the priority deadline. Early decision candidates must file their applications by December 1. Personal interviews are not mandatory; however, all candidates are urged to visit campus and interview if at all possible. Interviews can be scheduled between 8:30 A.M. and 4:30 P.M. on any weekday. On various Saturdays, the College hosts information sessions. Please contact Fisher for details.

To learn more or to receive an application, please contact:

Office of Undergraduate Admissions
St. John Fisher College
3690 East Avenue
Rochester, NY 14618
Telephone: 585-385-8064
800-444-4640 (toll free)
Fax: 585-385-8386
E-mail: admission@sjfc.edu
World Wide Web: www.sjfc.edu

SWEET BRIAR COLLEGE

SWEET BRIAR
COLLEGE

THE COLLEGE AT A GLANCE

Sweet Briar College is recognized nationally as one of the finest colleges for women in the country. Founded in 1901, Sweet Briar continues to attract bright, confident women with an innovative curriculum based in the liberal arts and sciences with strong programs in areas such as business, education, international studies, and environmental sciences.

Our students share a strong intellectual enthusiasm, an inquisitive spirit, a sense of curiosity, and powerful ambitions for the future. Sweet Briar's co-curricular opportunities for leadership, internships, service, and career planning guarantee our students' personal development. The highly qualified faculty, committed to undergraduate teaching of the highest standards, teaches individuals on a human scale. In small classes, students develop the knowledge, skills, contacts, and experience they want to fulfill their personal and professional aspirations in today's global society.

The College enrolls a diverse student body, with broad geographic, ethnic, and socio-economic representation; the approximately 600 students come from 35 states, 17 foreign countries, and every conceivable background. About 20 non-traditional-aged women are enrolled each year in the Turning Point Program.

LOCATION AND ENVIRONMENT

Sweet Briar is centrally located in Virginia, 12 miles north of Lynchburg and 50 miles south of Charlottesville and 165 miles southwest of Washington, D.C., on U.S. 29. The residential campus of 3,250 wooded acres is home to all full-time students except those in the Turning Point Program. The large proportion of faculty and administrators who also live on campus with their families enhances the community atmosphere of the College.

A blend of historical and contemporary buildings offers many attractions for visitors. The central campus, designed by the noted architect Ralph Adams Cram in the early part of this century, is a National Historic District. Sweet Briar House, the eighteenth-century plantation home of the College's founders and home of the president of the College, is listed in the National Register of Historic Places and is a Virginia Historic Landmark.

Sweet Briar is centered in a rich historical area, surrounded by such sites as Thomas Jefferson's Monticello and Poplar Forest, Appomattox Court House National Historic Park, and Point of Honor and is near natural sites such as the Blue Ridge Parkway, Natural Bridge, Peaks of Otter, Luray Caverns, and Skyline Drive.

Because of Sweet Briar's proximity to Washington, D.C., a large number of students are able to serve as

political, legal, or public service interns. Students work there and elsewhere for U.S. senators and representatives, attorneys, and local political organizations.

FIELDS OF STUDY

Students may choose from 35 departmental and interdepartmental majors. Self-designed interdisciplinary majors are available, and a student may choose to double major.

Majors: Anthropology, biochemistry and molecular biology, biology, business and management, chemistry, classical studies, computer science, dance, economics, education, English, English and creative writing, environmental science, environmental studies, French, German/German studies, government, history, history of art, international affairs, Italian studies, liberal studies, mathematics, mathematical physics, modern languages and literature, music, philosophy, physics, psychology, religion, self-designed major, sociology, Spanish, Spanish/business, studio art, theater

Minors: Archaeology, film studies, Italian, law and society, musical theater, women and gender studies

Area Studies: Asian studies, European civilization, international studies, Latin American studies, women and gender studies

Pre-professional Programs: Business and management, engineering, law, medicine/health sciences

Exceptional academic offerings are underscored by:

- A student/faculty ratio of 8:1, a ratio that reflects our commitment to provide every student with a personal, meaningful education
- An average class size of 12
- A highly qualified faculty, 97 percent of whom hold the PhD or the terminal degree in their field
- Unlimited opportunities for student leadership
- An emphasis on the unique learning strengths and interests of women

The Department of Education also offers programs of study that prepare students for certification to teach in early-childhood, elementary, and secondary schools.

Sweet Briar has a chapter of Phi Beta Kappa and offers a four-year Honors Program.

FACILITIES AND EQUIPMENT

The new $10 million Student Commons completed in 2002 is an imaginative state-of-the-art facility that links student residences with services including enhanced dining facilities, an expanded Book Shop, the College post office, and campus student organizations.

The breathtakingly beautiful campus includes two lakes for fishing and swimming, an 18-station Parcourse Fitness Circuit, six nature sanctuaries, and an extensive network of trails for walking, biking, hiking, riding, and jogging.

Mary Helen Cochran Library, combined with three other libraries on campus, provides students with the largest private undergraduate college library in Virginia. The libraries provide access to a wealth of information databases and computerized research resources, including electronic journals and indexes.

The Guion Science Center provides up-to-date equipment for biology, chemistry, physics, psychology, and computer science. Examples include a new digital imaging scanning electron microscope; a nuclear magnetic resonance spectrometer (NMR); Fourier transform infrared spectrometer (FT-IR) and diode array UV/VIS spectrometer; a calculus computer lab with Pentium 133 systems, VGA color graphic adapters and monitors, printers, and projection panels.

Lane Auditorium in the Babcock Fine Arts Center is host to cultural and intellectual events such as student dance and theatre productions, the Babcock Season, and world-renowned speakers such as Maya Angelou.

The Daisy Williams Gym includes a 25-meter indoor pool, basketball and volleyball courts, Nautilus and Cybex weight-training equipment, a cardio-fitness center, and two dance studios. Located on campus are fields for hockey, lacrosse, and soccer as well as 14 tennis courts.

The Harriet Howell Rogers Riding Center, one of the nation's best college riding facilities, includes a large indoor arena with PERMA-FLEX footing, an oval ring, 60 box stalls, 3 outdoor rings, and 14 paddocks; schooling outside courses; and three additional teaching stations.

STUDENT ORGANIZATIONS AND ACTIVITIES

Among the advantages of a women's college are the unlimited opportunities for women to participate and assume leadership roles in many types of organizations and activities. Sweet Briar women have enough ideas and enthusiasm to support nearly 50 student-led and student-managed organizations—everything from art and musical groups to student publications and cultural awareness groups. Many students take part in volunteer service projects during school terms and vacations. Students are self-governed through the Student Government Association, and all subscribe to and support a strong Honor System.

Athletic competition at the varsity level is available in field hockey, lacrosse, riding, soccer, swimming, tennis, and volleyball. Sweet Briar is a member of the National Collegiate Athletic Association (NCAA) Division III and competes in the Old Dominion Athletic Conference (ODAC). Club sports include fencing, riding, and slow-pitch softball. Instructional sports include badminton, basketball, boating, canoeing, dance, fencing, golf, hiking, jogging, riding, softball, squash, swimming, and tennis.

OFF CAMPUS OPPORTUNITIES

Washington Semester: Sweet Briar students may spend a term at American University in Washington, focusing on the judiciary system, international development, American studies, or economic, foreign, or domestic policy determination.

7-College Exchange: Provides an opportunity for students from Sweet Briar, Hampden-Sydney, Hollins, Mary Baldwin, Randolph-Macon (Ashland), Randolph-Macon Woman's College, and Washington and Lee to spend a term or an academic year at one of the other colleges.

Tri-College Exchange: Expands course offerings so that students may take a course at Lynchburg or Randolph-Macon Woman's College if it is not available at Sweet Briar.

Study Abroad: Sweet Briar sponsors the Junior Year in France and Junior Year in Spain programs and has special relationships with universities in England and Scotland. Students may also study in Australia, Austria, Bermuda, the Czech Republic, Denmark, Germany, Greece, Ireland, Italy, Japan, Nepal, New Zealand, Poland, the Republic of China, and Tanzania.

TUITION, ROOM AND BOARD, AND FEES

For 2002–2003, tuition is $18,760, room and board is $7,660, and the student life fee is $150.

FINANCIAL AID

Sweet Briar offers a generous financial aid program to assist qualified students to attend. Approximately 90 percent of Sweet Briar students receive financial assistance. The College offers a variety of academic awards designed to recognize excellence in academic areas as well as leadership in community, civic, and school activities. These awards range from $1,000 up to full tuition.

ADMISSIONS PROCESSES AND REQUIREMENTS

Admission to Sweet Briar is selective and is based on the strength of a student's high school transcript, SAT or ACT scores, application recommendations and required essay, and additional extracurricular, leadership, and service activities. Early decision applicants should apply by December 1. Regular decision applicants should apply by February 1. Transfer applications for the sophomore and junior classes are due by July 1.

For additional information, students should contact:

Office of Admissions
PO Box B
Sweet Briar College
Sweet Briar, VA 24595
Telephone: 800-381-6142 • Fax: 434-381-6152
E-mail: admissions@sbc.edu
World Wide Web: www.sbc.edu
CEEB Code: 5634 • ACT Code: 4406

UNIVERSITY OF ARKANSAS

AT A GLANCE

The University of Arkansas is the original campus and flagship institution of the University of Arkansas system. Among the 45 institutions of higher learning in Arkansas, the University of Arkansas is the state's only "Doctoral/Research University–Extensive," as categorized by the Carnegie Foundation for the Advancement of Teaching. As such, the University of Arkansas is in the top tier of 150 major research universities among the nations 4,048 post-secondary institutions

Founded in 1871, the University of Arkansas is both the major land-grant university for Arkansas and the state university. The University of Arkansas is located in Fayetteville, a city presenting the vibrant cultural life that would be expected in any major university town.

DEGREES OFFERED

The University of Arkansas consists of eight schools and has more academic programs than many larger universities—219 academic degree programs at the baccalaureate, master's, and doctoral levels. The most popular majors are marketing, computer information systems, finance, childhood education, and psychology. UA's pre-med program is particularly strong; 98 percent of honors students who applied to medical school were accepted. In addition, the popular College of Engineering offers co-op partnerships for students.

The University encourages the expansion of students' educational experiences through study abroad. A limited number of scholarships and travel grants are available each year for these programs.

FACILITIES

The campus proper comprises 130 buildings and 345 acres. It rests on a former hilltop farm that overlooks the Ozark Mountains. Old Main, the University's signature building, has come to symbolize higher education in Arkansas, and is one of 11 campus buildings that have been placed on the National Register of Historic Places. U of A has 11 residence halls, and all freshmen are required to live in a residence hall, fraternity, sorority, or at home with parents.

TUITION, ROOM AND BOARD, AND FEES

The annual expense for 2002–2003 area is s follows: tuition for in-state students is $3,573 and for out-of-state students is $9,945. Required fees are $883. Room and board is $4,810.

Incoming freshmen from the neighboring states of Texas, Mississippi, Missouri, Oklahoma, Louisiana, and Kansas with a 3.0 GPA and an ACT of 24 or above can enroll at in-state tuition costs.

Twenty-five percent of incoming freshmen receive university scholarships ranging from $3,000 annually to full tuition, fees, room and board, and books. There are many need-based scholarships and grants offered, in addition to loan aid, work-study, and institutional employment. Of the freshman class, 76 percent receive aid, as do 73 percent of undergraduates overall. The average freshman grant is $3,268 and the average freshman loan is $2,951.

SPECIAL INTEREST SCHOLARSHIPS

Coca-Cola Minority Scholarship: The University of Arkansas, with an endowment from the Coca-Cola Foundation, has established a four-year Coca-Cola Foundation Scholarship for outstanding incoming ethnic minority freshmen who are Arkansas high school graduates. The scholarship is equal to the current University of Arkansas cost of education.

Minority Teacher Education Scholarship: available to minority students pursuing careers in teacher education.

Arkansas Geographical Critical Needs Teacher Scholarship Program: available to students of color pursing careers in teacher education.

TRMEP: Transition-Retention Minority Engineering Program awards a limited number of scholarships to its summer participants.

U of A Black Alumni Scholarship: need-based, renewable scholarship offered by Black Alumni of the U of A to cover incoming freshman tuition.

The 2001–2003 Financial Aid Resource Books for African Americans, Asian American, Hispanic American, and Native Americans are available for review the Multicultural Center.

For more information, contact the Scholarship Office at 479-575-4464 or the Financial Aid Office at 479-575-3806.

FACULTY

Teaching is a primary mission of the University of Arkansas. At this mainly residential campus, the faculty numbers 864, of which 94 percent are full-time and 92 percent hold either the doctorate or the terminal degree in their field. Sixty-three percent of the faculty are tenured. The student/faculty ratio is a manageable 16:1.

STUDENT RESOURCES

The student enrollment for fall 2001 was 12,818 undergraduates and 2,934 graduate and professional students. African American students comprise 6 percent of the student enrollment.

The Multicultural Center exists to enhance the academic experience at the University of Arkansas by preparing students for life in a pluralist society. The staff seeks to provide a "home away from home" for African Americans students; to provide an environment that promotes cross-cultural interaction; and to collaborate with the University community in providing educational, cultural, and social programs and resources to assist in the development and advancement of a diverse community.

The Office of Multicultural Student Services seeks to develop and use existing programs in providing for the social, cultural, and academic presence of students of color on campus. In addition, efforts are made to educated and sensitize the campus community about diversity, while providing resources to assist each individual and University department in acquiring the skills and knowledge needed to make the University campus a place that truly respects and appreciates diversity.

The Office of Multicultural Student Services, Office of Admissions, and the colleges' Minority Affairs Offices sponsor an orientation program for first-year students of color entering the U of A. The program includes an advising session, special interest group program, and Meet Your S.M.I.L.E.

Students Making It Lighter Everyday (S.M.I.L.E.) is a peer counseling group composed of upperclassmen with the primary function of being a resource for students of color. Each peer counselor is assigned a number of incoming freshmen students to whom they provide a continuous source of information and support as well as referrals to other services when desired.

SPECIAL PROGRAMS FOR STUDENTS OF COLOR

African American Studies Program (AASP): aids the development of the student as an individual and to prepare such an individual to be a responsible member of a multiracial society. The goal is to provide knowledge and understanding of the history, social organization, problems, and the current status of African Americans and their contributions to the American heritage.

Inspirational Singers: serve as ambassadors of song, specializing in gospel and spiritual music, and are a major recruiting factor for minority students through scholarships offered by the group.

University of Arkansas Association of Black Journalists: has co-sponsored debates involving campus campaigns, job fairs in the journalism department, and trips to regional job fairs.

The Black Student Association (BSA): is a student governing body wherein the progress of black students in every aspect of university life is first priority. The knowledge and experience through active participation with the many facets of the U of A is supported and encouraged through this body to create a nurturing and success-oriented environment for black students.

NAACP Chapter: advances the economic, educational, social, and political status of people of color and serves as the training ground for a new generation of American leaders.

In addition to the above organizations, each college/school at the University of Arkansas has an office designed to work specifically with students of color to support their successful enrollment in and graduation from that college or school.

CAREER SERVICES & PLACEMENT

The University Career Development Center provides an array of programs and services for University of Arkansas Studentsl, including career advising, career assessments, training in job search strategies, professional etiquette, resume preparation, and job interview skills.

ADMISSION

Entering freshmen applications will be reviewed on an individual basis. Grade point average, class rank, ACT or SAT scores, and evidence of a commitment to success will be used to determine admissibility. Freshman or transfer applicants with fewer than 24 transferable semester hours are must have 16 units of college preparatory curriculum. The percent of applications accepted is 89 percent, with 58 percent enrolled.

Applicants who have taken the required units of college preparatory courses and have a minimum high school grade average of 3.0 and an ACT of 20 (or SAT of 930) or better will be admitted automatically. However, many students will be admitted on the basis of individual review of their application portfolios. The admission decision will be based on evidence of the applicant's ability to graduate from the University of Arkansas.

Opening date for admission is mid-September. The priority deadline for admission and scholarships is February 15. The admission and scholarship notification date is April 15.

For more information, contact:

Telephone: 800-377-8632 or 479-575-5346
Admsissions website: http://admissions.uark.edu/
University website: www.uark.edu

UNIVERSITY OF VERMONT

AT A GLANCE

Standing in the shadows of the Green Mountains on the shore of Lake Champlain, the University of Vermont (UVM) blends the faculty/student relationships most commonly found in a small liberal arts college with the resources of a comprehensive university. With 7,500 undergraduates and 1,500 graduate students, the University of Vermont is not so large as to feel overwhelming or so small as to feel confining. It feels just right to our students.

UVM is located in Burlington, Vermont, a metropolitan area of approximately 130,000. The University's main campus sits on a hill nestled between Lake Champlain and the Green Mountains. Because of the natural beauty of its surrounding area and its many sporting and entertainment opportunities, Burlington has been named one of the nation's "Big Ten" college towns by Edward B. Fiske in his book *The Best Buys in College Education*.

MAJORS AND PROGRAMS OFFERED

The University of Vermont offers more than 90 undergraduate programs leading to the Bachelor of Arts and Bachelor of Science degrees. Many of these programs offer special concentrations. In addition, the University offers curricula and advising for pre-medical, predental, pre-veterinary, and pre-law students.

An accelerated BS/DVM program with Tufts School of Veterinary Medicine and a BA/JD program with Vermont Law School are available. A 3 +3 guaranteed admission to the Master of Physical Therapy program is available to a limited number of entering first-year students.

The following majors are available through the University's seven colleges and schools: agricultural and resource entrepreneurship°, animal science, anthropology, art education, art history, art studio, Asian studies, biochemical science, biochemistry°, biological sciences, biology, biomedical technology, botany, business administration (*accounting, entrepreneurship, finance, human resource management, international management, management & the environment, management information systems, marketing, production and operations management*), Canadian studies, chemistry, civil engineering, classical civilization, communication and international development°, communication sciences, community development & applied economics, computer science, computer science information systems, dietetics, early childhood education, economics, electrical engineering, elementary education (K-6), engineering management, English, environmental engineering°, environmental sciences, environmental studies, European studies, family & consumer sciences education, forestry, French, geography, geology,

German, Greek, history, human development & family studies, individually designed major, Latin, Latin American studies, mathematics, mechanical engineering, medical laboratory science, microbiology, middle level education, molecular genetics, music, music education, natural resources (*integrated natural resources, resource planning, resource ecology*), nuclear medicine technology, nursing, nutrition & food sciences, philosophy, physical education, physics, plant and soil science, political science, psychology, radiation therapy, recreation management, religion, Russian, Russian/East European studies, secondary education (*English, language, mathematics, science, social science*), social work, sociology, Spanish, statistics, sustainable landscape horticulture, theatre, wildlife fisheries and biology, women's studies, and zoology.

°New for students applying for fall 2003

Students in the College of Arts and Sciences may also complete minors in African studies, ALANA studies, Asian languages, film studies, gerontology, Italian, Italian studies, Middle Eastern studies, speech, statistics, and Vermont studies.

OFF-CAMPUS OPPORTUNITIES

Walk a few blocks from main campus and you're in the heart of downtown Burlington. Bookstores, boutiques, department stores, restaurants and cafés line Church Street Marketplace, a lively pedestrian mall. Coffeehouses and music clubs about town feature rising stars, while the Flynn Center for the Performing Arts attracts national acts on tour.

Home to many businesses—from Burton Snowboards to IBM—Greater Burlington is Vermont's economic hub. UVM students gain hands-on experience as valued interns and volunteers with business, government, school, health care and other area organizations.

FACILITIES

UVM's 425-acre main campus includes Bailey/Howe Library, the Robert Hull Fleming Museum, Royal Tyler Theatre, 150 classrooms, 84 teaching laboratories, 24 residence halls, and the Patrick/Gutterson athletic complex, and is adjacent to the Fletcher Allen Medical Center. Off-campus facilities include four research farms, nine natural field study areas, and the Rubenstein Ecosystem Science Center.

Inside UVM's historic halls and modern buildings students find facilities that are state-of-the-art. UVM's library system offers full-text databases, an extensive catalog of films, videos, maps and government documents, as well as access to regional and national databases. Network links are provided in every residence hall room (one port per pillow), and over 700 terminals are available for student use.

AFFORDING A UVM EDUCATION

The University is interested in helping every student with the ability and desire to attend the University of Vermont to achieve that goal. UVM's admission policy is need-blind. In administering financial aid, the cost of attendance and calculated family contribution are considered. A student's academic record may also be taken into account. Over half of our students receive some form of need-based financial aid.

The University of Vermont participates in all federal student aid programs and sponsors its own programs to supplement federal and state assistance. Grants are also available to Vermont students through the Vermont Student Assistance Corporation. Out-of-state students are encouraged to contact their state's grant agency.

Merit Scholarships are available to first-year applicants whose academic strength, leadership, personal background, commitment to service, and potential to offer significant contributions to the campus community are considered in determining eligibility.

Tuition costs for the 2002–2003 are $21,450 for non-residents of Vermont and $8,960 for Vermont residents. Room and board is set at $6,400.

FACULTY

Over 89 percent of our faculty holds a PhD or the highest degree in their field. UVM is a community where you'll find distinguished faculty working closely with undergraduates in classrooms, laboratories and out in the field, all committed to the pursuit of knowledge. And with a faculty/student ratio of 13:1, students find faculty accessible and interested in their pursuits.

STUDENTS

Our students come from throughout the US and many foreign countries. Unusual for a state-assisted university, 62 percent are from outside of Vermont. Students value the exceptional diversity of interests and backgrounds.

UVM students have a knack for leading busy, complete lives that strike a healthy balance between hard work and play. Service and social activism are proud traditions at our University, reflecting a spirit of individualism joined with public commitment that stands out at UVM.

Nearly 80 percent of students participate in more than 100 campus organizations. "Joining is easy," say our students, "choosing is the challenge."

ADMISSIONS

The University of Vermont seeks students who demonstrate strong academic ability as well as possess talents and personal character that will enrich our university community. Here are some of the indicators we use in evaluating an applicant's candidacy for admission: High school performance (rigor of course work, class rank, cumulative grade point average, and/or grade distribution); personal qualities and experiences, activities, honors and awards, and special interests; SAT I or ACT scores; writing ability as presented in application essays; recommendations from teachers, counselors, employers, or others.

SPECIAL PROGRAMS

UVM's Exchange Programs allow any student to study abroad at the University's in-state tuition rate. Options include Kansai Gaidai University, Hirakata, Japan; Wirtschaft Universtitat Wien, Vienna, Austria; University of Lapland, Finland; University of Belgrano, Buenos Aires, Argentina; University of Sussex, Brighton, England; and University of Western Australia, Perth, Australia. Other study abroad options allow access to programs in more than 80 countries.

Undergraduate research opportunities are available throughout the university. The Hughes Endeavor for Life Science Excellence (HELiX) is one example of a program for students in the sciences.

Honors opportunities are available from department-based honors courses to college-wide programs incorporating residential options, seminars, field study, and cultural and social activities. College-wide programs with residential options include the John Dewey Honors Program for arts and sciences and education students; the Aiken Scholars Program for students in the natural resources; and the Morrill Honors Program for agriculture and life sciences students.

Our Teacher Advisor Program (TAP) places first-year arts and sciences students in small, interactive courses in which the teacher also serves as each student's advisor.

Other programs and services include the ALANA Student Center, which provides support primarily to students of African American, Latino/a, Asian American, and Native American descent; the Learning Co-op and Writing Center, which offers tutorial services to students; and ACCESS, a resource center that provides support and assistance to students with physical or learning differences.

CAREER SERVICES & PLACEMENT

Our most recent survey of UVM graduates shows 99 percent are employed or enrolled in graduate school within a year of receiving their degrees; 86 percent report they are "satisfied" or "very satisfied" with their current positions. UVM Career Services received a 2001 "Program of the Year Award" from the National Association of Student Personnel Administrators for career service that begins the minute our students set foot on campus and extends throughout their lives.

CONTACT INFORMATION

For more information contact the Admissions Office.
The University of Vermont
194 So. Prospect St.
Burlington, VT 05401-3596
802-656-3370
Admissions@uvm.edu

WILLIAMS COLLEGE

PROGRAMS AND CURRICULUM

The Williams curriculum is designed to allow maximum flexibility within a framework that guarantees that students pursue a broad-based and holistic academic program. Taking 32 courses over eight semesters, Williams students complete one major of approximately 10 courses. Overall, three courses must be taken in each of the College's three broad distributions of programs and courses: Division I—Languages and the Arts, Division II—the Social Sciences, and Division III—Mathematics and the Natural Sciences.In addition to a focus on students and a dedication to great teaching, Williams offers several programs unique among its peer institutions.Based on the tutorial format of teaching at Oxford University, the Williams College Tutorial Program offers students the opportunity to engage in intensive study of a particular subject in a class comprised of one other student and a professor. These two-on-one classes, available in most departments, allow students to focus on writing, research, and oral presentation of their ideas, in addition to spending a semester on in-depth exploration of a particular area of interest. Students may also elect to spend their junior year studying abroad at Oxford University through the Williams Oxford Program.Each student must complete one course or project each January through the Winter Study Program. Winter Study courses are not graded and do not count toward major or distribution requirements, freeing students to explore areas of alternative interest or to try something entirely new. Students may choose to take a course on campus (such as Stained-Glass Window Making or Managing Nonprofits), to engage in internships or practica (such as teaching in New York City or shadowing a local surgeon), or to study abroad with a Williams professor (recent destinations have included Cuba, China, Greece, and Nicaragua). Winter study is also a good time to relax between semesters, to spend time with friends, and to get involved with one of the more than 160 campus organizations.Williams is home to the largest undergraduate science and mathematics research program in the country. More than 160 students remain on campus each summer, receiving $3,400 plus room and board to work in the labs, alongside their professors, on science or mathematics research. Topics range from genetics to number theory to astrophysics and quantum teleportation.

OFF-CAMPUS OPPORTUNITIES

Approximately 40 percent of each class will choose to spend all or part of their junior year abroad on one of over 150 programs offered around the world. Students receiving financial aid may apply that aid to an abroad program of their choosing. Students often spend the summer months participating in Williams-sponsored

Founded in 1793 in the heart of the beautiful Berkshire Mountains of northwestern Massachusetts, Williams is widely regarded as one of the world's finest liberal arts colleges. Coeducational, multicultural, worldly and ecumenical, Williams is a warm and supportive community of students and professors who work closely in a student-centered educational environment. Although Williams is a highly selective college, the campus atmosphere is decidedly noncompetitive. Academic life is governed by an honor code that sets a high standard of integrity. Under this code, professors encourage collaboration on problem sets, labwork, and study, enabling students to see their classmates as resources, not competitors. Williams considers student support, both academic and personal, among its chief institutional priorities, and prides itself on having among the highest graduation rates and the highest freshman retention rate among all liberal arts colleges.

CAMPUS AND LOCATION

Williams maintains a spectacular campus with over 100 buildings on 450 acres. A town of approximately 8,000, Williamstown is three hours north of New York City and two-and-a-half hours west of Boston. Our closest airport is in Albany, New York, approximately one hour's drive from campus. Students enjoy the 100 miles of hiking and biking trails within a five mile radius of campus, and often make use of Williams's 2,200 acre Hopkins Memorial Forest.

DEGREES OFFERED

Williams confers a Bachelor of Arts degree in 31 majors, each of which consist of 9–11 courses. Approximately 25 percent of students choose to double major. Additionally, students may elect to complete "concentrations." These clusters of 6–7 courses allow students to engage in areas of interest not represented by a full major.

MAJORS

Available majors are American studies, anthropology, art (studio, history, or combined), Asian studies, astrophysics, astronomy, biology, chemistry, Chinese, classics, computer science, contract major (self-designed major), economics, English, French, geosciences, German, history, literary studies, mathematics, music, philosophy, physics, political economy, political science, psychology, religion, Russian, sociology, Spanish, and theater.

FIELDS OF CONCENTRATION

Fields of concentration are African and Middle Eastern studies, African American studies, biochemistry and molecular biology, environmental sciences, neuroscience, science and technology studies, and women's and gender studies.

or Williams-supported internships. Fifty $3,000 grants are available each summer to students interested in nonprofit or unpaid summer internships or employment. Additionally, twenty $3,000 Mead grants are available to support students interested in public sector work. Many other students connect with alumni around the county or world for summer work, research, or mentoring.

FACILITIES

Facilities include 40 dorms (95 percent of upperclass rooms are singles), five dining halls, a recently completed $55 million teaching and research building for the sciences, and spectacular athletic facilities and fields. Construction is currently underway on a new 90,000-square-foot theater and dance center.

TUITION, ROOM AND BOARD, AND FEES

For the 2002–2003 academic year, tuition, room, board, and fees totaled $32,470.

EXPENSES AND FINANCIAL AID

Williams is fortunate to be one of very few schools with the financial resources to maintain a need-blind financial aid policy toward all of its applicants. Put simply, the College will not take financial need into consideration when making admission decisions. Students are admitted solely on the basis of merit and, once admitted, are guaranteed 100 percent of their demonstrated financial need. Williams' need-blind admission policy applies equally to citizens of all countries. Approximately 50 percent of our students receive financial aid; the average aid package for the class of 2005 was $22,600. The range of awards was $4,175–$35,880. Williams does not offer merit-based scholarships but will apply outside scholarships to reducing the government loan and campus job portions of the financial aid package.

FACULTY

The 263 men and women of the faculty have chosen Williams because they consider teaching and interacting personally with students to be the most important aspects of their profession. A student/faculty ratio of 8:1 and an average class size of 15 means that students are encouraged, even required, to do most of the talking in classes. Since Williams has few graduate students, professors teach all classes, grade all course work, and run all labs.

STUDENTS

The 2,100 men and women of Williams have in common a fundamental academic ability and a desire for excellence. Beyond that, they are a notably disparate group, representing an astonishing array of backgrounds and interests. The student body consists of approximately 27 percent American students of color; nearly 20 percent first-generation college students; and over 60 percent graduates of public high schools. Students represent 50 U.S. states, 30 religious denominations, and 40 countries throughout the world. About half receive financial assistance. Beyond demographic diversity, Williams seeks students who will bring a wide variety of perspectives, talents, and passions to its community. As a result, Williams students fill 2 symphonies; 2 theater companies, 8 dance ensembles; 31 varsity and 14 junior varsity sports; 12 a cappella groups; 15 campus publications; a 24-hour radio station; more than 160 cultural, religious, and special-interest organizations; and a 900-member outdoors club.

ADMISSIONS

Admission to Williams College is highly selective. Each year, approximately 5,000 apply for 525 places.

To apply, students must submit the following:

- Completed application (Common Application is welcomed)
- Secondary school report
- SAT I or ACT results, plus any three SAT II results
- Two teacher references
- Personal statement
- Optional supplemental materials (tapes, resumes, research briefs, etc.)

CAREER SERVICES AND PLACEMENT

Reaping the benefits of a powerful liberal arts education, Williams students enjoy medical school acceptance rate of 90+ percent and a rate of 99+ percent to business and law schools and to science and mathematics PhD programs. More than 150 employers—banking and consulting firms, teacher placement agencies, nonprofit organizations and others—come to campus each fall to recruit seniors. Employers

and graduate schools know that a Williams graduate will be an intelligent and capable person, with the writing, critical thinking, and problem solving skills to excel in any field. Within 10 years of graduation 65 percent of Williams students earn a professional, master's or doctorate degree. Within a lifetime, the number is close to 80 percent.

FOR ADDITIONAL INFORMATION

Students wanting more information about Williams College should contact:

Director of Admission
Williams College
33 Stetson Court
Williamstown, MA 01267
413-597-2211 (phone)
413-597-4052 (fax)
www.williams.edu
wso.williams.edu
admission@williams.edu

ABOUT THE AUTHORS

Thomas LaVeist, Ph.D., is associate professor and director of the Center for Health Disparities Solutions at Johns Hopkins University, where he conducts research and teaches courses in the Department of Sociology and the Bloomberg School of Public Health. Before coming to Baltimore, Dr. LaVeist was a research associate at the Program for Research on Black Americans of the Survey Research Center of the Institute for Social Research at the University of Michigan. He has a doctorate in medical sociology from the University of Michigan. Dr. LaVeist is also a 1984 graduate of the University of Maryland Eastern Shore. In 1989, his dissertation was selected as the "Best Dissertation in Medical Sociology" by the American Sociological Association, and he was appointed a fellow at the Brookdale Foundation in New York. Dr. LaVeist has published extensively on health issues among African Americans, the meaning and health consequences of race and racism, and the effects of social factors on the health of populations. He has published numerous articles in scientific journals as well as newspapers and magazines. He lives in Baltimore, Maryland, with his wife Bridgette and his four children Carlton, Randall, Naomi, and Clay.

Will LaVeist is an accomplished journalist and executive for BlackVoices.com, a Tribune Company. He has worked in the newspaper industry for the *Mesa* Tribune, The Fresno Bee, and *The Arizona Republic* in various positions such as copy editor, reporter, and online editor. As a reporter, Will covered various beats, including health, city government, crime, and education. In 1994, he received an Arizona Press Club Award for creative writing. Will has a bachelor's degree in English from Lincoln University of Pennsylvania and a master's degree in journalism from the University of Arizona. Originally from the Brownsville section of Brooklyn, New York, Will now resides in the Chicago area with his wife, Rita, and children Daniel, Joshua, and Coryn.

Graduate School Entrance Tests

Business School

Is an MBA in your future? If so, you'll need to take the GMAT. The GMAT is a computer-based test offered year round, on most days of the week. October and November are the most popular months for testing appointments. Most business schools require you to have a few years of work experience before you apply, but that doesn't mean you should put off taking the GMAT. Scores are valid for up to five years, so you should take the test while you're still in college and in the test-taking frame of mind.

Law School

If you want to be able to call yourself an "esquire", you'll need to take the LSAT. Most students take the LSAT in the fall of their senior year—either the October or the December administration. The test is also offered in February and in June. The June test is the only afternoon administration – so if your brain doesn't start functioning until the P.M., this might be the one for you. Just make sure to take it in June of your junior year if you want to meet the application deadlines.

Medical School

The MCAT is offered twice each year, in April and in August. It's a beastly eight-hour exam, but it's a necessary evil if you want to become a doctor. Since you'll need to be familiar with the physics, chemistry, and biology tested on the exam, you'll probably want to wait until April of your junior year to take the test— that's when most students take the MCAT. If you wait until August to give it a shot, you'll still be able to meet application deadlines, but you won't have time to take it again if you're not satisfied with your results.

Other Graduate and Ph.D. Programs

For any other graduate or Ph.D. program, be it art history or biochemical engineering, you'll need to take the GRE General Test. This is another computer-based test, and, like the GMAT, it's offered year-round on most days of the week. The most popular test dates are in late summer and in the fall. Take the test no later than October or November before you plan to enter graduate school to ensure that you meet all application deadlines (and the all-important financial aid deadlines) and to leave yourself some room to take it again if you're not satisfied with your scores.

Understanding the Tests

MCAT

Structure and Format

The Medical College Admission Test (MCAT) is a six-hour paper-and-pencil exam that can take up to eight or nine hours to administer.

The MCAT consists of four scored sections that always appear in the same order:

1. Physical Sciences: 100 minutes; 77 physics and general chemistry questions

2. Verbal Reasoning: 85 minutes; 60 questions based on nine passages

3. Writing Sample: two 30-minute essays

4. Biological Sciences: 100 minutes; 77 biology and organic chemistry questions

Scoring

The Physical Sciences, Biological Sciences, and Verbal Reasoning sections are each scored on a scale of 1 to 15, with 8 as the average score. These scores will be added together to form your Total Score. The Writing Sample is scored from J (lowest) to T (highest), with O as the average score.

Test Dates

The MCAT is offered twice each year—in April and August.

Registration

The MCAT is administered and scored by the MCAT Program Office under the direction of the AAMC. To request a registration packet, you can write to the MCAT Program Office, P.O. Box 4056, Iowa City, Iowa 52243 or call 319-337-1357.

GRE

Structure and Format

The Graduate Record Examinations (GRE) General Test is a multiple-choice test for applicants to graduate school that is taken on computer. It is a computer-adaptive test (CAT), consisting of three sections.

- One 30-minute, 30-question "Verbal Ability" (vocabulary and reading) section

- One 45-minute, 28-question "Quantitative Ability" (math) section

- An Analytical Writing Assessment, consisting of two essay tasks

  o One 45-minute "Analysis of an Issue" task

  o One 30-minute "Analysis of an Argument" task

The GRE is a computer-adaptive test, which means that it uses your performance on previous questions to determine which question you will be asked next. The software calculates your score based on the number of questions you answer correctly, the difficulty of the questions you answer, and the number of questions you complete. Questions that appear early in the test impact your score to a greater degree than do those that come toward the end of the exam.

Scoring

You will receive a Verbal score and a Math score, each ranging from 200 to 800, as well as an Analytic Writing Assessment (AWA) score ranging from 0 to 6.

Test Dates

The GRE is offered year-round in testing centers, by appointment.

Registration

To register for the GRE, call 1-800-GRE-CALL or register online at www.GRE.org.

Understanding the Tests

LSAT

Structure and Format

The Law School Admission Test (LSAT) is a four-hour exam comprised of five 35-minute multiple-choice test sections of approximately 25 questions each, plus an essay:

- Reading Comprehension (1 section)
- Analytical Reasoning (1 section)
- Logical Reasoning (2 sections)
- Experimental Section (1 section)

Scoring

- Four of the five multiple-choice sections count toward your final LSAT score
- The fifth multiple-choice section is an experimental section used solely to test new questions for future exams
- Correct responses count equally and no points are deducted for incorrect or blank responses
- Test takers get a final, scaled score between 120 and 180
- The essay is not scored, and is rarely used to evaluate your candidacy by admissions officers

Test Dates

The LSAT is offered four times each year—in February, June, October, and December.

Registration

To register for the LSAT, visit www.LSAC.org to order a registration book or to register online.

GMAT

Structure and Format

The Graduate Management Admission Test (GMAT) is a multiple-choice test for applicants to business school that is taken on computer. It is a computer-adaptive test (CAT), consisting of three sections:

- Two 30-minute essays to be written on the computer: Analysis of an Argument and Analysis of an Issue
- One 75-minute, 37-question Math section: Problem Solving and Data Sufficiency
- One 75-minute, 41-question Verbal section: Sentence Corrections, Critical Reasoning, and Reading Comprehension

The GMAT is a computer-adaptive test, which means that it uses your performance on previous questions to determine which question you will be asked next. The software calculates your score based on the number of questions you answer correctly, the difficulty of the questions you answer, and the number of questions you complete. Questions that appear early in the test impact your score to a greater degree than do those that come toward the end of the exam.

Scoring

You will receive a composite score ranging from 200 to 800 in 10-point increments, in addition to a Verbal score and a Math score, each ranging from 0 to 60. You will also receive an Analytic Writing Assessment (AWA) score ranging from 0 to 6.

Test Dates

The GMAT is offered year-round in testing centers, by appointment.

Registration

To register for the GMAT, call 1-800-GMAT-NOW or register online at www.MBA.com.

Dispelling the Myths about Test Preparation and Admissions

MYTH: If you have a solid GPA, your test score isn't as important for getting into a college or graduate school.

FACT: While it is true that admissions committees consider several factors in their admissions decisions, including test scores, GPA, work or extra-curricular experience, and letters of recommendation, it is not always true that committees will overlook your test scores if you are strong in other areas. Particularly for large programs with many applicants, standardized tests are often the first factor that admissions committees use to evaluate prospective students.

MYTH: Standardized exams test your basic skills or innate ability; therefore your score cannot be significantly improved through studying.

FACT: Nothing could be farther from the truth. You can benefit tremendously from exposure to actual tests and expert insight into the test writers' habits and the most commonly used tricks.

MYTH: There are lots of skills you can learn to help you improve your math score, but you can't really improve your verbal score.

FACT: The single best way to improve your verbal score is to improve your vocabulary. Question types in the verbal reasoning sections of standardized tests all rely upon your understanding of the words in the questions and answer choices. If you know what the words mean, you'll be able to answer the questions quickly and accurately. Improving your critical reading skills is also very important.

MYTH: Standardized exams measure your intelligence.

FACT: While test scores definitely matter, they do NOT test your intelligence. The scores you achieve reflect only how prepared you were to take that particular exam and how good a test taker you are.

Hyperlearning *MCAT Prep Course*

The Princeton Review Difference

Nearly 40% of all MCAT test takers take the exam twice due to inadequate preparation the first time. **Do not be one of them.**

Our Approach to Mastering the MCAT

You will need to conquer both the verbal and the science portions of the MCAT to get your best score. But it might surprise you to learn that the Verbal Reasoning and Writing Sample are the most important sub-sections on the test. That is why we dedicate twice as much class time to these sections as does any other national course! We will help you to develop superlative reading and writing skills so you will be ready to write well crafted, concise essay responses. And of course, we will also help you to develop a thorough understanding of the basic science concepts and problem-solving techniques that you will need to ace the MCAT.

Total Preparation: 41 Class Sessions

With 41 class sessions, our MCAT course ensures that you will be prepared and confident by the time you take the test.

The Most Practice Materials

You will receive more than 3,000 pages of practice materials and 1,300 pages of supplemental materials, and all are yours to keep. Rest assured that our material is always fresh. Each year we write a new set of practice passages to reflect the style and content of the most recent tests. You will also take five full-length practice MCATs under actual testing conditions, so you can build your test-taking stamina and get used to the time constraints.

Specialist Instructors

Your course will be led by a team of between two and five instructors—each an expert in his or her specific subjects. Our instructors are carefully screened and undergo a rigorous national training program. In fact, the quality of our instructors is a major reason students recommend our course to their friends.

Get the Score You Want

We guarantee you will be completely satisfied with your MCAT score!* Our students boast an average MCAT score improvement of ten points.**

*If you attend all class sessions, complete all tests and homework, finish the entire course, take the MCAT at the next administration and do not void your test, and you still are not satisfied with your score, we will work with you again at no additional cost for one of the next two MCAT administrations.
**Independently verified by International Communications Research.

ClassSize-8 *Classroom Courses for the GRE, LSAT, and GMAT*

Small Classes

We know students learn better in smaller classes. With no more than eight students in a Princeton Review class, your instructor knows who you are, and works closely with you to identify your strengths and weaknesses. You will be as prepared as possible. When it comes to your future, you shouldn't be lost in a crowd of students.

Guaranteed Satisfaction

A prep course is a big investment—in terms of both time and money. At The Princeton Review, your investment will pay off. Our LSAT students improve by an average of 7 points, our GRE students improve by an average of 212 points, and our GMAT students boast an average score improvement of 92.5 points—the best score improvement in the industry.* We guarantee that you will be satisfied with your results. If you're not, we'll work with you again for free.**

Expert Instructors

Princeton Review instructors are energetic and smart—they've all scored in the 95th percentile or higher on standardized tests. Our instructors will make your experience engaging and effective.

Free Extra Help

We want you to get your best possible score on the test. If you need extra help on a particular topic, your instructor is happy to meet with you outside of class to make sure you are comfortable with the material—at no extra charge!

Online Lessons, Tests, and Drills

Princeton Review *ClassSize-8* Courses are the only classroom courses that have online lessons designed to support each class session. You can practice concepts you learn in class, spend some extra time on topics that you find challenging, or prepare for an upcoming class. And you'll have access as soon as you enroll, so you can get a head start on your test preparation.

The Most Comprehensive, Up-to-Date Materials

Our research and development team studies the tests year-round to stay on top of trends and to make sure you learn what you need to get your best score.

*Independently verified by International Communications Research (ICR).

**Some restrictions apply.

Online *and* LiveOnline *Courses for the GRE, LSAT, and GMAT*

The Best of Both Worlds
We've combined our high-quality, comprehensive test preparation with a convenient, multimedia format that works around your schedule and your needs.

Online *and* LiveOnline *Courses*
Lively, Engaging Lessons
If you think taking an online course means staring at a screen and struggling to pay attention, think again. Our lessons are engaging and interactive – you'll never just read blocks of text or passively watch video clips. Princeton Review online courses feature animation, audio, interactive lessons, and self-directed navigation.

Customized, Focused Practice
The course software will discover your personal strengths and weaknesses. It will help you to prioritize and focus on the areas that are most important to your success. Of course, you'll have access to dozens of hours' worth of lessons and drills covering all areas of the test, so you can practice as much or as little as you choose.

Help at your Fingertips
Even though you'll be working on your own, you won't be left to fend for yourself. We're ready to help at any time of the day or night: you can chat online with a live Coach, check our Frequently Asked Questions database, or talk to other students in our discussion groups.

LiveOnline *Course*
Extra Features
In addition to self-directed online lessons, practice tests, drills, and more, you'll participate in five live class sessions and three extra help sessions given in real time over the Internet. You'll get the live interaction of a classroom course from the comfort of your own home.

ExpressOnline *Course*
The Best in Quick Prep
If your test is less than a month away, or you just want an introduction to our legendary strategies, this mini-course may be the right choice for you. Our multimedia lessons will walk you through basic test-taking strategies to give you the edge you need on test day.

1-2-1 *Private Tutoring*

The Ultimate in Personalized Attention

If you're too busy for a classroom course, prefer learning at your kitchen table, or simply want your instructor's undivided attention, *1-2-1* Private Tutoring may be for you.

Focused on You

In larger classrooms, there is always one student who monopolizes the instructor's attention. With *1-2-1* Private Tutoring, that student is you. Your instructor will tailor the course to your needs – greater focus on the subjects that cause you trouble, and less focus on the subjects that you're comfortable with. You can get all the instruction you need in less time than you would spend in a class.

Expert Tutors

Our outstanding tutoring staff is comprised of specially selected, rigorously trained instructors who have performed exceptionally in the classroom. They have scored in the top percentiles on standardized tests and received the highest student evaluations.

Schedules to Meet Your Needs

We know you are busy, and preparing for the test is perhaps the last thing you want to do in your "spare" time. The Princeton Review *1-2-1* Private Tutoring Program will work around your schedule.

Additional Online Lessons and Resources

The learning continues outside of your tutoring sessions. Within the Online Student Center*, you will have access to math, verbal, AWA, and general strategy lessons to supplement your private instruction. Best of all, they are accessible to you 24 hours a day, 7 days a week.

*Available for LSAT, GRE, and GMAT

The Princeton Review
Admissions Services

At The Princeton Review, we care about your ability to get accepted to the best school for you. But, we all know getting accepting involves much more than just doing well on standardized tests. That's why, in addition to our test preparation services, we also offer free admissions services to students looking to enter college or graduate school. You can find these services on our website, *www.PrincetonReview.com*, the best online resource for researching, applying to, and learning how to pay for the right school for you.

No matter what type of program you're applying to—undergraduate, graduate, law, business, or medical—**PrincetonReview.com has the free tools, services, and advice you need to navigate the admissions process.** Read on to learn more about the services we offer.

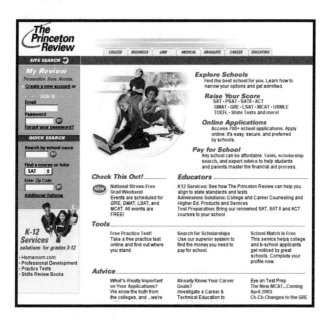

Research Schools
www.PrincetonReview.com/Research

PrincetonReview.com features an interactive tool called **Advanced School Search.** When you use this tool, you enter stats and information about yourself to find a list of schools that fit your needs. From there you can read statistical and editorial information about thousands of colleges and universities. In addition, you can find out what currently enrolled college students say about their schools.

Our **College Majors Search** is one of the most popular features we offer. Here you can read profiles on hundreds of majors to find information on curriculum, salaries, careers, and the appropriate high school preparation, as well as colleges that offer it. From the Majors Search, you can investigate corresponding Careers, read **Career Profiles**, and learn what career is the best match for you by taking our **Career Quiz**.

Another powerful tool we feature is **School Match**. You tell us your scores, interests, and preferences and Princeton Review partner schools will contact you.

No matter what type of school or specialized program you are considering, **PrincetonReview.com has free articles and advice, in addition to our tools, to help you make the right choice.**

Apply to School
www.PrincetonReview.com/Apply

For most students, completing the school application is the most stressful part of the admissions process. PrincetonReview.com's powerful **Online School Application Engine** makes it easy to apply.

Paper applications are mostly a thing of the past. And, our hundreds of partner schools tell us they prefer to receive your applications online.

Using our online application service is simple:

- Enter information once and the common data automatically trans fers onto each application.
- Save your applications and access them at any time to edit and perfect.
- Submit electronically or print and mail in.
- Pay your application fee online, using an e-check, or mail the school a check.

Our powerful application engine is built to accommodate all your needs.

Pay for School
www.PrincetonReview.com/Finance

The financial aid process is confusing for everyone. But don't worry. Our free online tools, services, and advice can help you plan for the future and get the money you need to pay for school.

Our **Scholarship Search** engine will help you find free money, although often scholarships alone won't cover the cost of high tuitions. So, we offer other tools and resources to help you navigate the entire process.

Filling out the FAFSA can be a daunting process, use our **FAFSA Worksheet** to make sure you answer the questions correctly the first time.

If scholarships and government aid aren't enough to swing the cost of tuition, we'll help you secure student loans. The Princeton Review has partnered with a select group of reputable financial institutions who will help **explore all your loans options**.

If you know how to work the financial aid process, you'll learn you don't have to **eliminate a school based on tuition.**

Be a Part of the PrincetonReview.com Community

PrincetonReview.com's **Discussion Boards** and **Free Newsletters** are additional services to
help you to get information about the admissions process from your peers and from The Princeton
Review experts.

Book Store
www.PrincetonReview.com/college/
Bookstore.asp

In addition to this book, we publish hundreds of other titles, including guidebooks that highlight life on campus, student opinion, and all the statistical data that you need to know about any school you are considering. Just a few of the titles that we offer are:

- Complete Book of Business Schools
- Complete Book of Law Schools
- Complete Book of Medical Schools
- The Best 345 Colleges
- The K&W Guide to Colleges for Students with Learning Disabilities or Attention Deficit Disorder
- Guide to College Majors
- Paying for College Without Going Broke

For a complete listing of all of our titles, visit our **online book store**:

http://www.princetonreview.com/college/bookstore.asp